Praise for

THIN ON TOP

"*Garratt, a leading UK authority on corporate governance, does not mince his words. Thin on Top does exactly what it says on the cover. It strips the board's functions down to their legal basics, offering simple knowledge tests on those, which he claims most directors fail. This ignorance, he argues, too often allows chief executives to 'bet the business'.*
His definitions of the three core board values - probity, transparency, accountability-should be on every director's desk.
So should this book."
Carol Kennedy, Director

"*Bob Garratt sets out in this timely book just how far modern business has strayed from first principles. The author has an impressive track record in this field. His earlier works* The Fish Rots from the Head *and* The Learning Organisation *marked Garratt out as one the most perceptive and grown-up observers of the business world. In this new book Garratt reaffirms the true duties and responsibilities of company directors, and suggests new approaches to measure and boost board performance.*

Whatever size company you are leading, Garratt's unflinching analysis makes for essential reading.This book is a challenge thrown down to the business community: do you really understand - and can you justify - the way your business is being run?

Don't read this book for comforting words or an easy life. But if you are serious about leading your business on to a healthy and robust future, get hold of a copy right away."
Stefan Stern, Business Voice

"There is more to governance than mere rules, a point that is interestingly explored by Bob Garratt in a new book which emphasises the human aspects of governance. Garratt, who has advised on governance across the world, argues that too much of the discussion focuses on the 'hard' and easily debated issues of compliance rather than the 'soft' but more difficult qualities of human vision, values and board performance.

He believes that the competence required by directors in the boardroom is very different from what is required of executives and under-trained direction-givers. Like Higgs, Garratt is keen to see a more rigourous approach to board training and appraisal."

John Plender, Financial Times

"This is the book for you. Behind it there is good sense. Garratt's main thesis is straightforward. He believes that most directors are ill-prepared for the roles they are required to play; that many have only the vaguest understanding of the board's duties; and that few receive any training that might usefully correct these deficiencies. And, he argues, boards are weak on assessing management, and particularly derelict in their duty to assess their own performance.

I suspect he is not far from the truth. He is certainly right to point out that boards that are guilty as charged face a rude shock as they move to full implementation of the Turnbull Code, and begin to explore the implications of whatever emerges as the final version of the Higgs recommendations on the role of non-executive directors. Those boards would do well to consider some of the recommendations - generally sensible - that make up the second half of Garratt's book. He has useful things to say about how to train and develop directors, how boards should interact with management and how to evaluate a board's own performance."

Howard Davies, Management Today

Thin on Top

Why Corporate Governance Matters
and How to Measure and Improve
Board Performance

Bob Garratt

NICHOLAS BREALEY
PUBLISHING

LONDON
YARMOUTH, MAINE

Dedicated to my godson
Adam Hay
1989–2002

First published by
Nicholas Brealey Publishing in 2003
Reprinted in 2004

3–5 Spafield Street
Clerkenwell, London
EC1R 4QB, UK
Tel: +44 (0)20 7239 0360
Fax: +44 (0)20 7239 0370

PO Box 700
Yarmouth
Maine 04096, USA
Tel: (888) BREALEY
Fax: (207) 846 5181

http://www.nbrealey-books.com
http://www.boardperformance.com

ISBN 1-85788-319-5

Library of Congress Cataloging-in-Publication Data

Garratt, Bob.
    Thin on top : why corporate governance matters and how to measure and improve board
performance / Bob Garratt.
      p. cm.
    Includes bibliographical references and index.
    ISBN 1-85788-319-5 (alk. paper)
    1. Corporate governance. 2. Boards of directors. 3. Financial disclosure--United States.
4. Corporations--Corrupt practices--United States. I. Title.

HD2741.G37 2003
658.4'22--dc21

2002044062

British Library Cataloguing in Publication Data
A catalogue record for this book is available from the British Library.

Printed in Finland by WS Bookwell.

Contents

Acknowledgments

S O MANY PEOPLE HAVE INFLUENCED AND constructively criticized my thinking and work over the past 25 years and across five continents that it is impossible to thank everyone. However, I must try, and the following have been especially helpful in helping me shape this book. The process started with the foresight of Lucinda McNeile in asking me to write the book for HarperCollins. Then in the ways of a turbulent world HarperCollins put its list on the market while I was writing and, with an astonishing lack of business nous, left it there swinging in the wind for many months. I was grasped warmly by Nicholas Brealey Publishing and had new energy and criticism at just the right time from Nicholas and Angie Tainsh, plus good text editing—that most thankless of tasks—from Sally Lansdell.

My colleagues at Board Performance Ltd—Clive Morton, Mike Bett, Jesper Berggreen, Jonathan Charkham, Sally Garratt, Des Gould, and Heather Matheson (none of whom is backward in coming forward)—have been consistently critical, usually constructively, and I thank them for it. To the debating process in the UK I must add Louise Barrett and Rosie Miller of Success Group, Chris Pierce, Peter Hammonds, Peter Humphrey, and John Harper, through the Institute of Directors, Michael Gillibrand at the Commonwealth Secretariat, David Bacon, Bernard Taylor at Henley, Sue Birley and David Norburn at Imperial College, Lord Peter Goldsmith, the members of AMED's Director Development Network, and Guy Jubb at Standard Life. I give my special thanks to those long-term supporters of my work Max Boisot, Sir Adrian Cadbury, Charles Handy, Bob Monks, Bob Tricker, and Reg Revans.

In East Asia I have many thanks to give to my colleague Peter Barrett at Organisational Development Ltd, Hong Kong; Ram Ramakrishnan and Maria Li at Organisational Development, Singapore; the committee members of the Singapore Institute of Directors and Loizos Heracleous; Dato Pengiran Ismail Mohamed and

Andy Shie in Brunei. In Australia the impressive Denise Fleming has been a long-time friend and critic; in New Zealand Ron Hamilton, Jane McCann, and Geoffrey Bowes have all helped greatly. In Southern Africa Logan Chetty, Boyman Mancama, Phil Armstrong and Richard Wilkinson have supported me strongly, as have my colleagues in the Saudi Arabian Monetary Agency and the Institute of Chartered Accountants, Bahrain.

In Europe Renate Psenicka of the Commission of the European Union, Margareta Hult (who let me have the wonderful Villa Gabrielle in Tourrettes-sur-Loup to write the book) and Ojvind Norberg in Sweden, Anne Naylor and Daniel Cohen in France, Jose-Maria D'Anzizu in Catalonia, Charles Minor in Amsterdam, and Hans-Joachim Spreng and Martin Harder have all helped by asking the sort of questions that require rather carefully considered answers. In the US the charge has been led by Roxanne Decyk at Shell and Lew Watts at Halliburton, both in Houston, Alexander Keyserlink and Anne Simpson in Washington, John Carver, and Peter Gorer and Chris Argyris in Boston.

My apologies to all I have missed. In the end I take full responsibility for my writing. I just hope that the reader finds it holds up to the demanding values of corporate governance: accountability, honesty, and openness.

Bob Garratt
London
February 2003

Foreword
by Bob Monks

BOB GARRATT IS THE IDEAL PERSON to write about corporate directors in today's world. That he has long warned us of most of the problems now appearing everywhere daily is part of his appeal; the rest, frankly, is that he has a gift for words and fears no one in his insistence on honest analysis.

It is the right time for this book. In the US, Michigan Senator Carl Levin, as chairman of an investigating committee, recently issued a careful and detailed report condemning the conduct of the board of directors of Enron Corporation and laying at their feet the blame for the losses suffered by investors, pensioners, and employers.

The Enron board failed to safeguard its shareholders and contributed to the collapse of the seventh largest public company in the US, by allowing it to engage in high-risk accounting transactions, with inappropriate conflicts of interest, extensive undisclosed off-the-books activities, and excessive executive compensation.

Levin's report followed eight hours of testimony and questioning of five of the principal directors, chairs of the important board committees. These individuals represented the *beau ideal* of American directorship—dean of Stanford Business School, CEO of three listed corporations, distinguished investor, Harvard Corporation member, director of the most famous medical institute, and so forth. They had experience and they were well compensated—$350,000 in the year 2000—but none of them accepted responsibility for the corporation's failure. It is plain that there exists a good deal of disagreement about the proper role and responsibilities of nonexecutive directors in the US.

At the same time, there is a vast amount of activity in the field of corporate governance in the UK. In implementing the Myners' Report into institutional investment the UK government has filled a vast gap by making clear what constitutes the role and responsibility of *shareholders*. A further inquiry led by corporate financier Derek Higgs is designed to reach a clearer definition of the role of "nonexecutive" directors. Nevertheless, although American triumphalism during the 1990s invites an appropriate response, the headline of CBI director-general Digby Jones' piece in the *Wall Street Journal*—"Needed: British-Style Capitalism"—may be a touch inappropriate. Americans are prepared to look at the unfortunate consequences of their actions, blemishes and all. Where, one might ask, is the Marconi Commission? Or is corporate governance wisdom in the UK to be communicated uniquely in the sweat-less confines of distinguished committees?

Bob Garratt is the right person to have written this book and we are all fortunate in the timing of its publication.

Robert A G Monks
Cape Elizabeth, Maine

The Future for Boards

Incarceration or Professionalization?

THIS BOOK ARGUES THAT THERE ARE fundamental differences between "managing" and "directing" an organization and that most current "board directors" are in reality merely rebadged managers. It argues that the present global corporate governance crisis in the private and public sectors is a complex mixture of directoral ignorance, strategic incompetence, and greed. It argues that a key to resolving the present crisis is to induct, train, and appraise directors as true professionals and to accept the intellectual, moral, and behavioral consequences of this. And it argues that unless such a systematic upgrading of directoral competence and board performance is undertaken, then the West's economic and political systems will rapidly erode, with serious consequences for its global power.

The crisis in corporate governance in western democracies has occurred because the roles, tasks, and accountabilities of the board of directors are not understood by politicians, business executives themselves, or the general public. As a direct consequence, public confidence in the markets, especially in the beneficial driving forces of the "equity culture," is being destabilized. We are seeing the end of one era of capitalism. People are seeking answers as to what should come next, but finding few. I believe that developing effective corporate governance and board performance is a key part of the solution.

I argue that until we see the board director role being professionalized and the supremacy of the board being reasserted, we shall not restore full confidence in either our business or public leaders or the markets. We need to ensure a system of board director selection, training, development, values, annual appraisal, and *self*-regulation, which will add the same type of rigor around the boardroom table as is often found further down the business. In short, we must learn how to measure and reward *directoral*, as distinct from executive, competence. It is no longer sufficient to assume that friends of the chairman[1] or CEO, pliant executives from other companies, or the great and the good will automatically make effective directors. Loosely defined "experience" alone is necessary, but not sufficient, for a place around the boardroom table. Only regularly assessed directoral competence will do, which will be painful for many existing and aspiring board members to acquire.

It is an open secret that the vast majority of directors are not fully competent. This is not to say that they are all therefore incompetent, but rather that most have not been able to distinguish between *managing* a business and *directing* one. They tend to be over-trained as executives and under-trained as direction-givers. Their many rewards have come from being effective professionals or managers, not from giving strategic direction. As board directorships come so late in most of their careers, it does not occur to many that they will have to retrain to become a competent director.

This mixture of ignorance and arrogance is both dangerous and paradoxical. It separates directors and top executives from their shareholders, yet it does so at a time when the investor base is widening dramatically to take in the much larger capital funds flowing from, for example, the working population's pension schemes, privatization shares, and life policies. With the current woeful under-performance of stock and other markets, compared with the rise and rise of executives' pay, these ordinary investors want to ask many more questions about the competence of directors and of their very well-paid advisers.

A Crisis in Corporate Governance

Over the last 25 years I have become increasingly angry about the lack of quality in corporate governance around the world, but I felt I had been one of a few small voices crying in the wilderness. However, now investors, politicians, and the general public alike have shown themselves to be unhappy with the lack of quality, integrity, and basic competence in boards of directors and with their messy and unprofessional relationships with shareholders, executives, and the wider social community of stakeholders.

When such notable names as GE, Johnson & Johnson, AOL, Merck, and Xerox are under scrutiny for their accounting practices; when Enron, Andersen, WorldCom, Tyco, and Adelphia are indicted for alleged criminal wrong-doing, with some top executives carted off in handcuffs; and when companies as seemingly respectable as Marconi, Equitable Life, Vivendi, or Kirch are apparently capable of strategic incompetence by betting the business on a single strategy and failing with incredible speed, then something is fundamentally rotten with western capitalism as we have known it. There is a growing loss of public trust in the governance of our corporations, private and public, and in the politicians who are meant to create the regulatory mechanisms by which they should be controlled. Today's public mood reinforces Lord Thurlow's maxim that "corporations have neither the bodies to be punished nor souls to be condemned; they therefore do as they like."

The business community in both the US and the UK is increasingly accepting that overblown optimism and greed have led to the present dismal situation, and that a return to basic business values is crucial to restoring the public's confidence through ending the era of the "celebrity CEO." What are these values? For over 400 years good governance, public or private, has been built on three fundamental corporate values:

❖ Accountability.
❖ Probity (honesty).
❖ Transparency (openness to the owners).

These have been reinforced from the time of America's Founding Fathers onwards by the basic personal, human values of:

❖ Humility.
❖ Honesty.
❖ Trust.
❖ Frugality.
❖ Quality.
❖ Accountability.

In modern times these are the values espoused for over 30 years by that wisest of company chairmen and investors, Warren Buffett, chairman of Berkshire Hathaway. He is the antithesis of the Gordon Gecko, "greed is good" culture of the 1980s and 1990s.

When Alan Greenspan, Chairman of the US Federal Reserve, says that the 1990s can be summed up by the term "infelicitous greed," following his long-famed criticism of the "irrational exuberance of the markets" and their "outsized increase in the opportunities for avarice," then you know that the pressure is on to change the prevailing values. Business has listened as much to Greenspan as to any US President. Many business leaders now accept that they have blown the opportunities for adding true long-term shareholder value, as distinct from ramping up the current share price out of self-interest.

Nevertheless, the violence of the public and political reaction against excessive corporate greed and corruption has led to offending senior US executives facing 20-year jail sentences for mis-stating their quarterly accounts, when the average term for even murder is 12 years. This suggests an absurd scenario where a US CEO with wrongly declared quarterly figures might be better bumping off the company's chief financial officer, for which the penalty is likely to be 12 years in jail, rather than going down for 20 years for misdeclaring their quarterly accounts. Or put another way, the current political response is unbalanced and risks creating more social destabilization by failing to realize that rushed reforms could lead to severe economic and social problems, as they turn off the very wealth creators needed for our society to develop.

I am worried that the term "corporate governance" itself has become highly fashionable and is, therefore, likely to become devalued rapidly by overuse. It is today's hot topic and I am very aware that business writing is a fashion industry. For example, when I wrote *The Fish Rots from the Head* in 1995 the phrase corporate governance was not in common use. Now you cannot avoid it, and it is in danger of being seen as the silver-bullet answer to all public and private policy and strategic problems. Inevitably it is not a universal panacea and it may eventually be thrown aside, despite its crucial importance in ensuring board performance, which I discuss in detail later in this book.

My business experiences—ranging from London to the streets of Northern Ireland, China in the Cultural Revolution, seeing the start of the crumbling of Zimbabwe, the uncertainty inside Saudi Arabia and the Arabian Gulf, and the rise and fall of the Asian Tigers—have moved me over time from a William Morrisian socialist/craftsmanship view of the world to a (grudging) acceptance of George Orwell's praise of the democratic bourgeoisie as the stabilizing strength in any liberal society.

In 1976 I experienced simultaneously both the tough, financially driven philosophy of General Electric under the late Lord Weinstock, and the authoritarian, and much disliked, Maoist government of the People's Republic of China in Beijing during the Cultural Revolution. Trying to make sense of the underlying governance, values, and organizational truths of such extreme and diverse political, economic, and social systems helped clarify for me the idea that all effective long-term human organizations are based on those three well-tested values underpinning all good governance, national or corporate.

I realized that business owners need simple, robust systems for monitoring, appraising, and actively criticizing the governance and leadership of organizations operating in their name. It did not matter whether I was working with the harsh but fair financial discipline of GEC's famous seven financial ratios and twelve trend lines or the perversities of Marx's labor theory of value, it was the thoughtful, humane, and wise exercise of power by direction-givers and the subsequent generation of trust, or distrust, among the owners, staff, and other stakeholders that determined the organization's effectiveness and efficiency. At that time GEC triumphed and Maoism failed miserably.

From Board Conformance to Board Performance

This book delves much deeper than the present headline issues. It sets the problems of corporate governance in historical, economic, and psychological perspectives. In the first half it reflects on both the fundamental causes of the failings of corporate governance—lack of board conformance and ineffective board performance—and then in the second half the focus is on positive actions that are being taken to resolve the global crisis in directoral competence.

The book deals with the big issues of ownership, power, control, and corruption in corporations about which pro- and anti-capitalists are in heated debate. But rather than adopting a strongly right-wing, left-wing, or nihilist stance, I take a pragmatic, libertarian view, derived from some 30 years of working with boards of directors in five of the six continents; South America still eludes me. I am interested in which governance systems work in any political environment, the generic structures, processes, and values that lead to effective boards, and the consequent development of a civil society.

I start with the observation that there are fundamentally *human* aspects to all governance issues, because effective direction-giving is ultimately a matter of judgment. I am interested particularly in what happens "behind the boardroom door,"[2] through the interacting dynamics of those powerful egos who are charged with the fundamental dilemma of directing—how to drive their enterprise forward while keeping it under prudent control. Their sense of balance can go seriously wrong on occasion unless there are robust and confident individuals around the boardroom table capable of independent thought and criticism and willing to blow the whistle if things get out of line. Without such people, bad board decisions can quickly become not just a local or a regional issue but one of global importance both politically and economically.

In the second half of the book I draw out best practices for effective corporate governance, addressing always the fundamental directoral dilemma of dynamically balancing board performance with board conformance. Good corporate governance is not just complying with the rules in a formulaic way, but is about the board's *performance* contributing to the direction, health, and wealth of the organization. I cover such aspects as the ten duties of a director, the necessity of full triple bottom line accounting, the development of learning boards, and the use of directoral dashboards for measuring and monitoring performance. These deal with the human actions "behind the boardroom door": building directoral competence to ask probing questions of powerful people; developing personal strategic thinking; and playing a truly collegial role as a direction-giver.

Most of the current international debate on corporate governance has not been about improving board performance and shareholder value at all, but on such relatively arcane issues as agency theory, voting rights, and the drafting of yet more regulatory legislation. All of these are aimed at improving the "hard" (and easily debated) issues of board conformance/compliance, rather than the crucial "soft" (and difficult to debate generically) aspects of the specific mix of human vision, values, and behavior that leads to performance for a particular board. The board conformance arguments are becoming so focused and intense that they increasingly resemble those medieval disputes about how many angels can stand on the head of a pin. Board *conformance* is necessary but not sufficient. Sufficiency comes from wealth generation through effective board *performance* within the law, for the propagation of sustainable civil societies.

The dangerous combination of a lack of understanding among directors of their specific duties of trust, care, and learning, plus the insidious corporate myth that the first duty of a board of directors is to its shareholders, often leads boards astray and thus into the open hands of over-powerful and frequently selfish chief executives. This book is written to help counter such corporate and psychological abuse and to go further by opening up the world behind the boardroom door in such a way that the general public will be able to demand that all boards adhere to their professional duties.

Part I

Behind the Boardroom Door

CHAPTER ONE

The Delaware Delusion

Three Myths of Corporate Governance

I N THE FIGHT FOR THE FUTURE of Hewlett-Packard during the merger talks with Compaq, Walter Hewlett made impassioned pleas, sadly unfulfilled, for US boards of directors to be prised away from over-reliance on the chief executive's ideas and information base, so that the directors could deliver their proper "fiduciary duty" to ensure the future health of their company.

How to deliver this fiduciary duty of directors—to hold the company in trust for the future—is at the core of this book. I am attempting to rebalance the corporate seesaw so that Adam Smith's notion of capitalism developing naturally, with a strong "moral sentiment" as its counterpoint, comes back into play.

My argument is that a truly radical return to the very roots of the western systems of business and government developed over the past 250 years will pay great dividends in terms of both value creation and social justice. A key foundation for such a business renaissance is the establishment of an internationally accepted system of corporate governance, building on those three values of accountability, probity and transparency.

Defining Corporate Governance

As western democracies struggle toward more open and accountable government, we see corporations failing to respond to the simultaneous and growing public demands for more effective "corporate governance." But what precisely do we mean by that?

I define corporate governance as:

the appropriate board structures, processes and values to cope with the rapidly changing demands of both shareholders and stake-holders in and around their enterprises.

Many businesses have not yet made the intellectual connection between the demands of shareholders and those of their stakeholders, those individuals and groups who have the power of sanction over board actions, usually through social legislation. If anything, boards have turned their backs on both and so created some stupidly perverse reward systems, especially for executives. We have over-praised celebrity chief executives and over-rewarded the clever boys of financial engineering. As their financial instruments and accounting become more and more complex to stretch the liquidity of the markets, we seem to be reaching a point of *reductio ad absurdum*. Baffled board directors, owners, and the public retreat into an ignorant silence leaving board decision-making to CEOs and financiers, while hoping for the small warmth of some *Schadenfreude* at their likely subsequent fall from grace. As the Australians say of their tall poppies, "They have to grow high before we can cut them down. But then it is a national sport to do so." This is limited relief when measured against reduced personal and national wealth caused by directoral incompetence or fraud.

In good times both the cream and the scum rise to the top. Very few people are willing to blow a warning whistle when everyone seems to be winning in a rising market. When that market turns and the cream curdles, however, the scum becomes only too obvious. What looked to the public like marvelously engineered marble palaces turn out to be two-dimensional lath and canvas film sets, loosely held together by "creative," EBITDA accounting. It is only after the downturn that most directors and senior executives begin to realize the difference between being clever and being wise—and by then it is too late for them not to be held personally, and corporately, liable.

An anonymous email circulating in London in 2002 sums this up well:

Normal capitalism: you have two cows and buy a bull. Your herd multiplies and the economy grows. You sell the bull and retire.

Enron capitalism: you have two cows. You sell three of them to your publicly listed corporation, using letters of credit opened by your brother-in-law at the bank. You then execute a debt/equity swap with an associated general offer so that you get all four cows back, with tax exemption for five cows. The milk rights of the six cows are transferred via an intermediary to a Cayman Islands company, secretly owned by your chief financial officer, who then sells the rights for all seven cows back to your listed corporation. Your annual report states that your corporation owns eight cows, with an option on six more.

As well as greed for seemingly easy returns leading to market volatility and confusion, matters are made worse by the huge rise in litigation against boards and individual directors caused by shareholder distrust, and the consequent massive increases in directors' and officers' liability insurance premiums. Worse, more and more experienced directors are unwilling to take the personal risks now associated with fulfilling their board duties. Good executives no longer want the exposure of the top jobs and are happier to stay at the "marzipan layer," workforces are increasingly demoralized by corporate under-performance, individuals feel disempowered and poorer, and many of the younger generation are emotionally against "big business." This is the unhealthy environment in which western democracies began the twenty-first century.

It is time to return to basics, to remember what companies are for, to allow market forces to flow to optimize value creation and distribution. We need to reaffirm and rigorously apply laws on the existing duties, liabilities, roles, and tasks of boards of directors. The tough application of these alone would prevent most of the directoral disasters we read about in our newspapers every day. And as well as fostering board conformance, we need to measure and boost board performance.

Three Myths of Corporate Governance

There are three powerful and widely held organizational myths that get in the way of improving corporate governance:

1 The myth of the all-powerful chief executive

Many chief executives believe that they "own" the organization that employs them and so have *carte blanche* to do whatever they wish with it. This is not so. Managing directors and chief executives are not free agents and are directly accountable to the board of directors and ultimately, through them, to the shareholders. They have an absolute duty to exercise care in their proposals and actions, and to hold the company "in trust" for future generations. Many boards blunder through their corporate life not appreciating these duties, having no systems for monitoring conformance with them, and giving all their trust to the chief executive in the naïve hope that he or she at least understands what is required. Thus many CEOs get away with surprisingly little competence and few if any appraisals. Meanwhile, many directors and executives see it as a career-limiting decision to challenge any CEO's abuse of the directoral duties of care and trust, so bad CEOs continue to thrive and exercise remarkable levels of personal power.

Unless the chief executive is also the majority shareholder, the normal legal process in most countries is that the owners appoint the board of directors. Then the board appoints the chairman of the board of directors. The directors also appoint the managing director (who by legal definition is on the board) or chief executive (who is not). This simple sequence is currently honored more in the breach than the observance, out of ignorance on both owners' and directors' sides.

2 The myth that a director's primary duty is to the shareholders

The second major myth of corporate governance is that the primary duty of a director is to the shareholders. This is not the case at law. In most jurisdictions with a developed system of commercial law—including the US, UK, and Commonwealth—at the very moment of a director's appointment to the board their primary loyalty switches from those who appointed them to the company itself, as a separate legal personality.

Although developed in the seventeenth century by the East India Company, the concept of "boards of directors" really came into its own in the nineteenth century. They were seen as putting a brake on the excesses of both the owners and the managers. They were designed to act as intelligent buffers between the two parties, to test the strategies of the managers, and to police the executives' stewardship of the company's scarce resources. However today most directors, private and public, are appointed quite incorrectly as "representatives" of the owners, lenders, staff, trade unions, or pressure groups. This often puts them in direct, if unwitting, conflict with their corporate and personal legal liabilities. The argument is that if the directors ensure the safety and long-term prosperity of the company, then by definition the interests of the shareholders are assured. They, and the board as a whole, must exercise this duty of care to hold the company in trust for the future and to insure against any short-term demands by the shareholders that may kill the company.

Again, this fundamental notion of the prime loyalty of a board being to the company as a separate legal personality is usually honored more in the breach. But if that is the case, there are usually dire consequences for the organization and the board itself in the long term. These can only be countered by the combination of a wise chairman; a board of directors dedicated to using their individual and collegiate capabilities for critical review, risk assessment, and unbiased, honest decision-taking in the best interests of their company; and a competent company secretary to ensure that they obey the annual legal rhythm demanded by the law.

3 The myth of executive and nonexecutive/independent directors

The third myth is that there are two types of directors, executive and nonexecutive. This is not true. In case-law countries the only term used is director, and even then much of the description of the director's role is found in the Insolvency Acts rather than company law. The key assumption is that of directors acting together as a group of equals around the boardroom table charged with driving the enterprise forward while keeping it under prudent control.

This legally collegiate view of a board of directors implies that all directors, as distinct from executives, are effectively part-time. Yet they are crucial for the business and so need to be seen, to be paid, and to act as equals. Therefore, they should all be paid the same director's fees, with any misnamed executive directors being paid a separate fee quite apart from their executive salary. This helps all of them focus on understanding that directing is a very different job from managing, for which they are paid separately. They must, therefore, budget time to be inducted, developed, and appraised, if they wish to become and remain effective directors. In turn, possessing such competence helps limit their exposure to personal liability and so protects their own, their family's, and the corporation's wealth.

The Delaware Delusion

The attitude prevailing in the US is a good illustration of the three myths of corporate governance in action. There appears to be a split personality in relation to "big business." On the one hand there is a deep and well-proven belief in the freedom of markets, their ability to generate significant and rising wealth, and their potential for social good. On the other hand there is a growing chorus of criticism that a tiny élite of business and financial executives are so distanced from the majority of the population, and so obsessed with their own celebrity and greed, that they are on a collision course with economic and social reality and, most importantly, with the general, more altruistic and religious values of the wider population.

Part of US corporate folklore is the belief in the paramount importance of the rough, tough, all-powerful chief executive who creates new markets, cuts costs ruthlessly, sees trade unions as for wimps, and is paid hugely. If they are successful, many minor infringements of good governance and the law, and holding some debatable personal values, are not only forgiven but celebrated publicly. This is usually measured only by rising share prices. The preference of directors to register their companies under the accommodating laws of the State of Delaware has helped reinforce this stereotype. But is the Delaware delusion about to be challenged by the US public in pursuit of safer pensions and equities, the return to basic human values, and the consequent demand for retribution from failed corporate leaders?

Why Delaware? Around half of the Fortune 500 companies are registered there. It has been a welcoming state for US corporations that want to seek the protection of its "business-friendly" courts. These have allowed such notions as the "poison pill" (a strategy used by a corporation to discourage a hostile takeover by making its stock less attractive to the potential acquirer) and the "just say no" defense to a hostile takeover. And it has become rich by offering such protection. A very comfy reciprocal understanding has been built, reinforcing what is now seen as the worst aspect of corporate governance—the over-reliance on executive management's sagacity and a consequent belief in the relative stupidity of shareholders. Delaware became an international byword for an over-comfortable relationship between the state and corporations at the expense of the shareholder.

However, even in Delaware this is changing, as the direness of US corporate governance practices is sinking into the public's awareness. To the consternation of many CEOs and chief financial officers, the State of Delaware has recently made a number of rulings against corporate executives. It has done away with the "dead hand" poison pill defense that (astonishingly) continued to operate even when all the board had been sacked. It has even overturned bylaws that made it difficult to sack a board. The five judges of Delaware's Court of Chancery, based on medieval English law, have also been taking a more "investor-friendly" approach. In particular, they have begun to place some faith in the notion that institutional investors should be treated as "sophisticated investors." They have begun to take an interest in the idea of independent directors and the voting power of shareholders. And in mid-2002 the judges sat for the first time to debate corporate governance issues with some of the largest institutional investors.

Are we seeing a true *mea culpa* repentance? Not yet. Nell Minow of LENS[1] has been tracking what is happening in Delaware and has expressed regret over a recent Court of Chancery ruling in favor of Hewlett-Packard, which had been accused of buying shareholders' votes to speed its merger with Compaq. Her disgust is seen in her words "the rulings are filled with good rhetoric but the decisions still go the other way." She wants "shareholder suffrage" to be as hallowed by the public as is the right to vote in the US Constitution. Her skepticism is warranted.

However, I feel that we are beginning to see a significant shift in US corporate life and especially business values. President George W Bush appears belatedly to have recognized that things have gone too far and a tough political response is required. In July 2002, addressing a worried Wall Street audience, he restated his fundamental belief that "the American economy is the most creative and enterprising and productive system ever devised," but then seemed to go against his instinctive support of big business at any price and said, "American newspapers should not read like a [business] scandal sheet. Too many corporations seem disconnected from the values of our country." He acknowledged that the existing civil and criminal laws should be better enforced and that "we must usher in a new 'era of integrity' in corporate America." Rather than put yet more rules on to corporations, his approach seemed to focus on protecting shareholders by reinforcing their abilities to protect their own interests. He is aiming to do this in three ways:

❖ Reinforcing the role and powers of auditors and making it a criminal offense for executives and directors to mislead them.
❖ Strengthening the role of "independent" directors as overseers of executive performance.
❖ Taking a much firmer stance on ensuring that executives' pay is linked directly to performance, and that stock options are accounted for as costs rather than allowed to linger off the balance sheet.

Nevertheless, what Bush did not address in any systematic way was the need to assess the competence of US directors; nor the scandal that in 2001 only 20 percent of Fortune 500 chief financial officers were Certified Public Accountants, as a survey by Peter McLean of Spencer Stewart showed. Some 35 percent of them had MBAs and just 5 percent had both qualifications. In the UK if a finance director of a listed company did not have a professional financial qualification he or she would be laughed off the exchanges.

In July 2002 the Sarbanes-Oxley Act passed into law to rein in corporate governance and accounting excesses in the US and countries with secondary listings in the US. Interestingly, its main provisions try to face up to the three myths of corporate governance. They are:

❖ The creation of penalties for corporate fraud, including prison for up to 20 years for destroying or altering documents needed in federal investigations.
❖ Chief executives who certify false accounts face prison terms of between ten and twenty years, and fines of $1–5 million.
❖ A five-member, private-sector board to oversee the accounting profession, with disciplinary and *subpoena* powers.
❖ A restriction in the consulting and nonaudit services that accountancy firms can provide to clients.
❖ The Securities and Exchange Commission will impose new rules on financial analysts to clarify conflicts of interest, especially in investment banks.
❖ Extension of the time period in which defrauded investors can bring lawsuits.

These are in addition to the SEC ruling that senior executives must vouch for the probity of their accounts. If the legislation can be made to work, and if the criminalization of boards and executives can be treated with discretion, then they could have a positive major impact on changing global thinking on corporate governance. If not, then the destabilization of western economies will speed up.

Corporate Governance in the UK and the US

The UK is seen internationally as having led the field of corporate governance reform, especially director and board competence assessment and development. Cynics will argue that the UK simply made the big mistakes first and therefore had to do something about them or lose its international financial position. There is some truth in this. But the bigger picture shows that in the last ten years the UK has developed a robust national structure and process for both the board conformance and board performance aspects of corporate governance. This was being taken seriously, and globally, a decade before the failure of the Enron Corporation and other corporate collapses. It thus has the beauty of not being a political knee-jerk to an immediate crisis but a more carefully considered and integrated set of responses, led crucially by practitioners rather than politicians, which has been tested and refined.

It is significant that in early 2002, as the post-Enron crisis gathered pace, Paul Volcker, ex-Chairman of the Federal Reserve, made a plea to the Bush administration that it should immediately adopt the UK's accounting practices and study its corporate governance procedures. Samuel DiPizza, US CEO of accountants PricewaterhouseCoopers, repeated this call and asked that US accounting standards should at least mirror European Union rules if not the more rigorous UK ones. The desperate need for the reform of the US-GAAP accounting standards is now widely acknowledged internationally, although US political action, as distinct from rhetoric, is still slow. However, not everyone is happy with even modest reforms. Such demands can be interpreted as attacks on the US way of life and especially the US way of doing business. But isn't this what got us into the mess in the first place?

While there is little doubt that the US has been lax in its policing of corporate governance practice, the notion that its business model is obsolete is under heavy counterattack. Paul Volcker's plea was answered only days later at the Stern Business School by the current incumbent at the Federal Reserve, Alan Greenspan. It was a modern example of an old argument over the nature of business power and control. He harked back to Berle and Means' argument[2] from the 1930s that has become a political and cultural icon for much of US business: The strength of the US business model is in giving maximum power to a strong chief executive and then relying on the weakness of a fragmented shareholder base that can effectively exercise its criticism of the present executives only by selling its shares. Although acknowledging that corporate governance had evolved over the last century to promote the allocation of the nation's savings more effectively to its most productive uses, Greenspan also insisted that as corporations have grown and the shareholder base has become more dispersed, few now hold sufficient stakes to influence the chief executive, especially as the directors are usually chosen from a slate selected by that CEO; as are the auditors and the audit committee. He argued that this is how it should be—until the company is in difficulties. He insisted that this paradigm has worked well and that there is no realistic alternative, despite analysts (often so well disposed to the CEO that some are now facing trial for defrauding clients) persistently being "overly optimistic" about corporate performance and thus effectively lying to existing and potential shareholders.

Although there is talk, especially in continental Europe, of the dangers posed to the "social market model" by the "Anglo-Saxon model of corporate governance," the notion of there being a single, integrated Anglo/US governance model is untrue. US and UK corporate governance practices are significantly different—especially in their approach to compliance issues. The US is a highly "rules-based" system, with great emphasis placed on external agencies ensuring compliance and, if necessary, litigation. The UK is more based on "general principles" being spelled out nationally, and then more self-regulatory processes to ensure that everything necessary is taken into account to give a "true and fair" picture by the board to the company's owners. The presentation of such information is left to the board under a "comply or explain publicly" approach. There is a strong regulator—the Financial Services Authority or FSA—but also an acknowledgment that on occasion there can be compelling reasons for a variation in the general approach, as long as the reasons are made public in a timely manner, so that the owners can decide on the validity of the approach and take appropriate action.

Nevertheless, the underlying case law, business frameworks, and general approach to the identification and resolution of both business and political problems are sufficiently the same in the UK and the US for them to be treated in this book as of similar provenance and aspiration. This is especially true when compared with corporate governance models found on other continents, particularly the continental EU countries. Because the US is seen by many as the global role model in so many areas, its old, bad practices are still being copied by many companies and governments in other countries. When appropriate this book attempts to deconstruct and differentiate US and UK corporate governance practices and suggest better ways forward internationally.

US semantic and structural confusion

As we are dealing here with national and international mindsets, paradigms, and corporate cultural folklore, it is worth trying to clear the ground in terms of semantics. George Bernard Shaw was right in his comment on the UK and US as "two nations separated by a common language." From the 1860s onward US corporations and governments got themselves into a semantic and legal muddle over both executive and directoral job titles and their direction-giving structures. They are not in line with common law and cause confusion by, for example, using the word "director" twice—once as a member of the board of directors, and once as an executive position usually below the rank of vice-president. The title "director" truly belongs only to a board member and is thus protected in law. All the others are "executives" or "managers."

Life is made more difficult in the US by casual abuse of the titles "chief executive" and "president" when the notion of "managing director" and "chairman" has stood the test of time across the vast majority of the rest of the world. I suspect that the US confusion goes back to two related issues. First, during the American Civil War President Abraham Lincoln wrote of his fear that he had struck Faustian deals with Northern big business to ensure the *matériel* he needed to finish the war. His worry was that he had to concede so much economic and political freedom to business interests without appropriate control that they would later abuse these and so destabilize the growing United States. Coupled with the "opening up" of the US West, this led many owners/leaders of the emerging great corporations to see themselves as essentially beyond the remit of the state and federal governments. In this condition the title "president" is both attractive, authoritative, and a great boost to the ego—especially when there are few federal regulatory mechanisms to check any misdemeanors. However, such abuse of power is surely against the design of the original American Constitution, which sought to balance the different powers of the national legislature, judiciary, and executive carefully through strong regulatory mechanisms. I am still hoping to find the first US written reference to the use of the corporate title "president." Curiously, nowadays many US corporate presidents are charming and unempowered, all of their significant power having been devolved to the chief executive and the consequent growth in power of the executive vice-presidents.

This theme of concern over corporate monopoly power and its subsequent abuse against the interests of the public was reflected in a major speech by President Dwight D Eisenhower. In 1961 as he was leaving office, he said in relation to the Cold War and US business interests:

> *We have been compelled to create a permanent armaments industry of vast proportions. Added to this, three-and-a-half million men and women are directly engaged in the defense establishment. We annually spend more than the net income of all US corporations. This conjunction of an immense military establishment and a large arms industry is now in the American experience. The total influence— economic, political, even spiritual—is felt in every city, every state house, every office of the federal government...*
>
> *In the councils of government, we must guard against the acquisition of unwarranted influence, whether sought or unsought, by the military industrial complex. The potential for the disastrous rise of misplaced power exists and will persist.*

There is a second, and bigger, problem for US corporate governance: The current insidious, but long-established, habit of the chief executive officer—at law not a member of the board of directors—to insist on also taking the chairman of the board position, title, and pay package as part of his employment contract. This negates or abolishes any chance of the chairman exerting his crucial, and neutral, role in both overseeing board processes and supervising executives.

Without such a *self*-regulatory mechanism the corporation lays itself open to criticism by anti-capitalists. Adam Smith recognized the problem. While praising the radical intellectual breakthrough of the joint-stock company with a separate legal personality, he saw also that it had the potential to create social upheaval in the long term because there were no social mechanisms for checking its unlimited size, unlimited license, unlimited life, and consequently unlimited power.

Board Conflicts of Interest

As has become only too obvious recently following the furore over fraud allegations at such companies as Enron, WorldCom, Tyco, and Adelphia, in most western countries directors and executives have been able to rely with some confidence on their ability to behave incompetently, unethically, and sometimes illegally with only a small chance of retribution. The rottenness at the core of much present capitalism does not relate to the structure itself but rather to the cavalier way in which it is operated, and the unwillingness to enforce existing sanctions on those who break the rules. The laws are there, civil and criminal, but the public is ignorant of them—and who among the present players has an interest in blowing the whistle to bring them into operation?

A significant number of chairmen, managing directors, chief executives, and directors appear to believe that they are both invulnerable and have inherent moral rightness in their actions, even if some rules have to be broken in their unstinting pursuit of pushing up the share price. So "whistleblowing" employees are usually stamped on. Staff with stock options or linked pension schemes do not want to rock the boat, even when they know that things are wrong, for fear of wrecking the share price. Audit committees are often ciphers of the chief executive and are comprised of selected, passive "nonexecutive" directors. In addition, auditors often seem more interested in generating consultancy fees than in their proper role of being employed by the shareholders to give an accurate, disinterested account of the finances of the business. Security firm analysts know that too deeply critical reviews, and too many "sell" notes, can damage their company's linked investment banking opportunities, so they self-censor or, as recent indictments suggest, lie. Investors are usually kept in the dark about business strategies, risk assessments, and current performance. The regulatory authorities are often weak, slow, and politically pliant in their responses to compliance infringements, and the business media often have conflicting interests that block any deep investigation of financial wrongdoing.

So who has any interest in whistle-blowing? At the moment only groups of disaffected shareholders, pressure groups, and citizens with a sense of probity in public life. Could the development of effective, fully trained and self-policing boards of directors make a significant contribution to rectifying this international problem? I believe that the answer is "yes," but it will take sustained international cooperation to get there.

Conspiracy or Cock-up?

A theme of this book concerns what boards, directors, and executives can do themselves to break the current corporate misgovernance cycle, to make directors much more professional, to reduce corporate corruption, and so help to ensure that the rule of law drives us all toward a stronger social contract to reach the goal of a civil society.

Are the majority of directors, especially CEOs, really as clever, cynical, and unwise as I have made out? In my experience they are not. Yet, curiously, they often strive very hard to look so, in the misguided belief that this is how "business" must be. Such behavior leads to another fundamental, and currently fashionable, question: Are directors driven by underlying theories of conspiracy or cock-up?

If one is to believe many nongovernmental organizations, anticapitalist groups, eco-warriors, animal rights terrorists, and supporters of the antiglobalization movements, then there can be only one answer—conspiracy. And not just any conspiracy, but a global conspiracy of corporations and totalitarian governments determined to dominate the world. They see as proof of this the fact that of the 100 major economic entities in the world, at least 27 are unelected corporations rather than elected governments.

This is worth more than a moment's thought for two reasons. First, most western critics of corporations do not look closely at the governments to which they refer and ask whether the majority of those are properly elected. At present such questioning must include the United States. While corporations are not fully accountable in terms of electoral process, current national voting processes alone do not guarantee the promised land either.

Secondly, western shareholders do have the right to elect directors to work on their behalf. Few people seem to know this. The cynics will query this immediately, but owners do have a vote. That they are ignorant of this fact, and so rarely exercise it, is the fault of all of us. Moreover, the growing majority of these "owners" are not the famed bloated plutocrats of old but more the pension funds of those very workforces, retirees, and stakeholders on whose behalf the NGOs say, sometimes paradoxically and patronisingly, that they are campaigning.

As an aside, it is wise to question who democratically elects the executives of the NGOs; who gives them a clear remit for their actions; and who oversees and audits their corporate governance and performance? At best the picture is murky. At worst their power lies with a tiny handful of self-selecting peers. So NGOs are as prone to ineffective corporate governance with illusions of invulnerability and moral superiority, and consequent incompetent direction and ineffective management, as is any board of directors.

My experience of working internationally with government leaders, company chairmen and chief executives, NGOs, not-for-profits, and community groups is that the response to the "conspiracy or cock-up?" question is rarely simple. It is usually much more subtle and often contradictory. It is unwise and simplistic to expect a binary "either... or" answer to solve the world's evils. It is wiser to understand that a complex series of frequently changing "both... and" dilemmas will in future face all citizens living in a continuously turbulent environment. Included among the citizens are directors. They are paid to face dynamic directoral dilemmas concerning values, strategies, risk assessments, and corporate resource deployment. These need continuous monitoring, debating, balancing, and rebalancing by the board. An effective process for dynamic corporate governance is needed urgently and internationally.

Not only Conformance but Performance

When I entered the world of board and director development in 1974, the most surprising revelation for me was that there were no formal processes to ensure that directors and senior executives (and, I realized later, ministers, prime ministers, and national presidents) were trained to competence for their direction-giving role. Naïvely, I had assumed as a citizen that competence training was a given for anyone in a top leadership role in the private or public sectors. Surely there must be some agreed measure of competence, and some sort of rite of passage, because these jobs are obviously crucial for a healthy society?

As disillusionment began to take over, I was less surprised that there were no induction or inclusion processes for directors joining most boards, no training or development budgets for directors, nor any appraisal systems for directors or boards. All of these processes cut out well below such an exalted organizational level as it was assumed that such people did not need training. Something mysterious and unassessable called "experience" was deemed sufficient to get them through to their retirement.

However, I noticed that this "experience" was usually all managerial and professional, not directoral. Organizationally it was inward and downward facing, leaving few if any directors to face upward and outward to look at the evolving future of a changing world, and to be able to design their organization's place in it. I was faced with boards who had very few coordinates with which to orientate their directoral roles and tasks. They were, therefore, ignorant front-runners for the cock-up philosophy of directoral life.

Yet their critics did have a point. There was also clearly a conspiracy—not of global domination, but rather a conspiracy of silence. There was an observable, tacit agreement between directors not to mention that they were unskilled, or at best semi-competent, in their direction-giving role. This conspiracy was reinforced by the owners'—

whether citizens or fund managers—willingness not to probe this open secret. There might be many mutterings of discontent in the coffee room or at the hustings, but the truth should never be made public for fear of the personal and market consequences. Shareholders and the public had a naïve belief that people chosen to give direction must, on their very appointment, become omniscient and skillful. Surely, they reasoned, they must know what they are doing or they would not have been selected in the first place?

The evidence in this book will show that this assumption is largely false. Presidents, prime ministers, chairmen, and chief executives alike have said to me in private that they are unsure of exactly what they have to do to become proficient in direction-giving, or how to measure their effectiveness. So they do what human beings often do when ill at ease and regress to their position of comfort. They do those parts of the job with which they are already over-familiar—typically their previous job, whether executive or professional—leaving the rest of the work alone, hoping either that it will be covered by someone else or that no one will notice the gaps. Thus they are not doing the directoral job for which they were elected or selected, and for which they are being well paid. Importantly, by doing the job below that for which they are paid, they block the development of all the people below them. The consequence of this is that their entire organization is suboptimizing its performance, with obvious consequential loss to its shareholders and stakeholders.

Therefore it is vital that in addition to ensuring board conformance with best practices in corporate governance, we find ways of assessing and improving the performance and competence of boards and the directors that comprise them, as well as means of professionalizing the directoral role. First, in the next chapter I consider the reasons for the increasing international importance of corporate governance.

CHAPTER TWO

The Increasing Importance of Corporate Governance

Boards will be under much greater scrutiny in the future. Observing a board in action is an exercise in Heisenberg's Uncertainty Principle—it changes both that which is being observed and the observer—in both cases usually for the better.

Bob Monks and Nell Minow of LENS

The trouble with British boards is that they mark their own examination papers.

Lord Halifax

LORD HALIFAX'S DICTUM HAS PROVED HORRIBLY true, nationally and internationally, since he uttered it some 70 years ago. Bob Monks and Nell Minow are also highly prescient with their view of the future. From now on the performance of boards will be under much stricter and wider scrutiny on the part of at least seven different vested interests that I will describe in this chapter.

Why have we only recently been faced with a torrent of proposed changes in corporate governance and accounting standards, starting well before scandals such as Enron?

Losing the Charmed Circle

Until the late 1970s the number of US and UK shareholders was small and communications with them relatively easy, even informal on occasion. The Exchanges of the City of London and Wall Street were very much exclusive clubs with their consequent strengths and weaknesses, but where, remarkably, "my word is my bond"—controlled by a strong blend of individual conscience and the fear of being banned from the self-regulating club forever—still held sway. Trust was assumed to be absolute between parties to a transaction. Personal integrity was considered above mere corporate legality. Being thrown out of the club was the height of personal, and family, humiliation and degradation.

The geographical focus of both exchanges was clear: mainly the US and South America for Wall Street, and for the City of London mainly the UK and the Commonwealth. Continental Europe, Russia, Japan, and China were not well represented on either exchange, yet their big projects were worthy of finance. The financing of the Suez Canal, the railways in the UK, US, and South America, and the Australian and South African mining companies were characteristic of the more imaginative and speculative stocks of this period of imperial confidence, integrity, and risk-taking. They used a romantic model of capitalism that was highly successful in growing markets and funded both the Industrial Revolution and the recovery from two great wars.

Typically a director's working (office) days were short and lunches long, collegial, and often alcohol fueled. How things have changed. The mindset now is meant to be all numbers, regulation by law only, self-interest, ruthlessness, over-long hours, and mineral water and sandwiches at your desk. The levels of client service and comfort are now sufficient, but no more, to do the deal just within the law. Yet even deep into the era of the film *Wall Street* in the late 1980s, and well after the fashion for alcohol-free "lite" lunches was established, guests at the end of a serious City lunch with, say, Hill Samuel Bank were given four courses in a private dining room with waiter service and later, with their port, were presented with a piece of crystallized ginger in a scallop shell to remind all present of their Oriental beginnings and their early funding of the Shell company. If you were included in such august company, it could be a very comfortable life. Being a company director was a particularly happy part of it and gave you real standing in society—but *being* a director was much more important than the art of *directing*.

However, throughout history there has been a "shadow side" to being in trade or business. In many countries the role of traders and money lenders was frequently difficult and often proscribed. In ancient Chinese and Irish Celtic societies the trader was rated so low as to be only one rung above the night-soil collector and common laborer. In medieval times the notion of "craft" was developed to raise their status and begin to differentiate the more skilled artisans from the common crowd. Indeed, in London many craft guilds became wealthy City livery companies. Nevertheless, the taint of being called "trade" still has deep resonance in most societies and can be felt beneath the surface even today.

The doubtful reputation of business people as shifty, indolent, greedy, amoral, cold, and unfeeling has been reinforced frequently in literature. Shakespeare's Shylock is an obvious example, as are some of those encountered by the travelers in Dante's *Divine Comedy*. By Victorian times Dickens' Mr. Gradgrind epitomized capitalism red in tooth and claw, while Anthony Trollope in *The Way We Live Now* characterized some directors' propensity for a chilling mix of idleness and venality, with little thought of sustained hard work and even less of shareholders' interests. Augustus Melmotte's Great South Central Pacific and Mexican Railway Company board would rarely sit for more than 30 minutes. "Melmotte himself would speak a few, slow words ... always indicative of triumph, and then everybody would agree to everything, somebody would sign something, and the board ... would be over."

In more modern times Agatha Christie depicted being a director as a good excuse to come into town for lunch and shopping (but she did acknowledge that her boardroom had "nice blotting paper"). Even in Harry Potter there is a push for freedom by the house-elves from an obvious business magnate-style character.

When writers have tried to portray the good side of business it hasn't really worked well. David Lodge's *Nice Work* is wonderfully comic, but although the central business character, Vic Wilcox, is portrayed for a change as honest and hardworking, he is drawn as both culturally under-developed and terminally dull. The only modern book of which I am aware that even attempts to paint a brighter side is the ex-Soviet American Ayn Rand's 1957 novel *Atlas Shrugged*, and even then it is a middling piece of writing. The defining sentence is:

> *If you ask me to name the proudest distinction of Americans, I would choose—because it contains all the others—the fact that they created the phrase "to MAKE money". No other language or nation had ever used these words before; men had always thought of wealth as a static quantity—to be seized, begged, inherited, shared, looted, or obtained as a favor. Americans were the first to understand that wealth has to be created. The words "to make money" hold the essence of human morality.*

Even now, with a more financially literate population and a slowly growing understanding of the meaning of effectiveness in the board and director's role and the key competencies, directors are still not appreciated by the wider public.

Outside of the charmed Wall Street and City circles, in the "real world" life was always tougher and more turbulent. However, even until the 1980s becoming a director had an aspirational pull. It was seen as an easier and richer lifestyle for which little effort or expertise was needed. The managers made the daily business decisions and took all the necessary actions. Except in times of great crisis, the directors only took decisions by exception. This "binary power of directors"— simply to accept or reject the proposals of management—was quite a seductive job proposition. "Management proposes and the board disposes" became an unthinking chant of idle directors. Attending a board meeting once a month and nodding assent was considered by all sides to be quite sufficient to fulfill one's directoral duties and allow payment of one's director's fees.

As late as the 1990s it would have been seen by many directors as an act of gross indecency to suggest a number of propositions that are at the core of the present debate over the future governance of corporations. For example:

❖ That boards have a crucial and active role to play in the leadership of an organization.

- ❖ That they would need to understand the art of rigorous critical review of both policy and strategy proposals.
- ❖ That they need to be open and explicit to their owners on the nature of their risk-assessment and decision-making processes.
- ❖ That they would need to be capable of helping the executives implement, and learn from, their proposed business strategy.
- ❖ That they would need to undertake regular assessments of the board, and of each individual director's competence within it.
- ❖ That they would be held personally accountable for their decisions and actions.

Indeed, you would have been drummed out of the Establishment—club, regiment, or country—for even suggesting such heresies. Yet it is worth remembering that the notion of "corporate governance" has been around for a long time.

The term "governance" came originally from the Greek *kubernetes*, steersman, into Latin, then into Middle English via Old French. One of the first known references is in Geoffrey Chaucer's *Canterbury Tales*, in "The Nun's Priest's Tale" relating to the cock Chantecleer's "gouvernaunce" of his seven hens, his dungheap, and the farmyard (see the Notes for a modern rendition):

> *This gentil cok hadde in his gouvernaunce*
> *Sevene hennes for to doon al his pleasaunce.*

The final moral of the tale shows the danger of turning a blind eye to governance issues:

> *Thou shalt namoore, thrugh thy flatereye,*
> *Do me to synge and wynke with myn ye;*
> *For he that wynketh, whan he sholde see,*
> *Al wilfully, God lat him nevere thee.*
> *"Nay," quod the fox, "but God yeve hym meschaunce,*
> *That is so undiscreet of governaunce*
> *That jangleth whan he sholde holde his pees."*[1]

Is this the earliest English-language reference to the relationship between turning a blind eye to corruption and bad governance? It certainly reflects the modern concern with the effective governance values of accountability, probity, and transparency. Some cynics would say that the references to being king of the dungheap and dodgy marital relationships show that not much has changed over the centuries.

Bob Tricker wrote the first book on *Corporate Governance*[2] in 1983. This did a remarkably comprehensive job of mapping much of the field and remains a seminal book. Yet it still contained links to the widely held assumption, and debatable practice, that the central role of board activity was the hiring and firing of the chief executive. Apart from in the US, this is now increasingly becoming unacceptable as the core board activity, because it smacks of an essentially passive board with long periods of inactivity followed by a "binary decision" on executives' proposals. At the time the book was published the notion of *board conformance* (compliance to a code of conduct) was still being formed. The notion of *board performance* as a sustained, real-time role for directors was even further off.

The Shock to the Establishment

When Confucius' disciple Tsze-Kung enquired of the philosopher the essence of good government, the master replied:

> *You need three things—weapons, food, and trust. In times of trouble you should give up weapons first, then food. But you should never give up trust. Without trust we cannot stand.*

The shockwave that rocked the status quo for ever and propelled "corporate governance" to the fore around the globe was not Enron or the other scandals of the early 2000s. Rather, it started slowly in the 1980s when a series of corporate frauds and legal cases in the UK and the US shook the complacency of many boards and forced legislators into action, initially in the UK. The failure of such a historic British name as Rolls-Royce, plus the share support scandal in the Guinness affair and the plundering of Mirror Group pension funds by Robert Maxwell and his cohorts, all figured prominently in rattling the financial and political establishments—and did long-term damage to the public's trust in the probity and competence of boards and directors, and of their company pension funds.

As is the nature of the popular media, suddenly all directors were portrayed as fundamentally corrupt, ravening, greedy capitalists with only the increase of their personal wealth, through inflated salaries and stock options, foremost in their minds. Shareholder, pensioner, and stakeholder rights were seen to be of no importance to them.

The public did not like this, but had no easy way of understanding what was happening or of responding except by public demonstrations. Privatizations in the UK heralded the era of the overpaid "fat cats" and the ensuing public abreaction reinforced the country's push to the forefront of corporate governance reform. Some ridiculous, short-sighted, and self-serving behavior by the boards of these newly privatized businesses speeded the reform process. It seemed to the public that previously second-rate senior managers from nationalized industries were being promoted and over-paid as directors in their newly privatized companies—without training or any change in their competence, nor any processes for assessing their performance. They became directors simply because they were there, and in a few cases put up some small "risk" capital to reap some very under-valued assets.

To make matters worse, the new directors seemed to have no intention of doing anything to audit, assess, or improve their board, or their individual, competencies. The notion of performance-related pay was anathema to them, unless it was based on very weak and easily achieved targets. The media and public focused on their apparently unstoppable appetite to award themselves vast salaries and stock options while stretching everyone's credibility by claiming simultaneously that they were now part of a scarce world market for top executives. No comparators were given as evidence of this world shortage of competent direction-givers. And no one in the general public believed that there was a world market for second-raters.

Meanwhile, continental Europe continued with its "Rhenish model" of corporate governance with over-close relations—often interlocked at corporate and political levels—between government and big business to the disadvantage of electors, shareholders, and open markets. While such a system was meant to speed economic growth across the EU, it seemed to have the opposite effect. Combined with an aging population, an absurdly expensive Common Agricultural Policy, political promises to reduce the retirement age and working week across the European Union, and no obvious way of being able to continue to fund the pay-as-you-go national pension plans of France, Germany, Italy, Greece, Spain, or Italy, the EU began its long slide into irrelevancy and impoverishment, while maintaining fiercely that open capital markets and large-scale managed immigration were a bad thing.

Where Was the Board?

It was the Mirror Group pensions scandal of 1988 that really caught the public's imagination internationally and raised the fundamental corporate governance question of: "Where was the board?"

Robert Maxwell's illegal pillaging of the MGN pension funds to try to support his failing businesses is so well reported that I will not go into detail here. After his death (reputedly through falling off the back of his yacht while relieving himself at night) his sons, after an unacceptably long time delay, were finally exonerated from association with the criminal actions. Nevertheless, the trial's outcome left a very nasty taste in the public's mouth and caused the politicians to begin their traditional clamor that "something must be done."

Interestingly, they did not legislate nor demand an immediate "tick box" approach. The latter is more characteristic of the US obsession with "rule-based" control, where trust, discretion, and a broad overview are left at the door while a one-size-fits-all scheme is imposed.

Cadbury Report

The UK took a different, "comply or explain" approach post-Maxwell. In a very British way the route of voluntary regulation, with added transparency for the owners, was deemed worth trying before resorting to legislation and a "rules-based" approach—even in business the Brits still tend to trust people until proved otherwise. People of high probity, led by Sir Adrian Cadbury, were asked by the London Stock Exchange to form a committee to examine the financial aspects (only) of this new area called "corporate governance." This led to the now world-renowned 1992 *Report of the Committee on the Financial Aspects of Corporate Governance*,[3] which established the UK as the thought leader in the development of best practice for effective corporate governance.

The Cadbury Report also helped generate a "corporate governance movement," especially in Commonwealth countries such as Australia, Canada, New Zealand, and South Africa, plus the Netherlands, with the US tagging along behind, worrying more about investment-related aspects of corporate governance while enjoying a fast-rising stock market. France and Sweden were also-rans and the rest of the EU was out of the picture altogether.

These corporate governance movements were driven by two distinct purposes. First, to ensure tighter accountability of board members and individual directors to their owners for their actions. Second, to counter growing corruption in many companies (private and public) and countries, and so reinforce the movement to establish the rule of law, anti-money laundering, and (later) anti-terrorism practices, and thus the help the liberal democratic process toward its ultimate goal of a more global "civil society."

The first objective of tightening accountability is well underway in many countries. By implementing self-regulatory codes of best practice and then ensuring (at least for listed companies) that they must report to their owners through at the very minimum their annual report and accounts, progress is being made. If companies are not following best practice they also have to explain why and be accountable to their owners for so doing.

The Cadbury Report had a remarkably positive impact internationally and its best-practice recommendations are now found across the globe, especially in the 54 Commonwealth countries. These are being applied increasingly not just to listed companies but in many private companies, public service organizations, charities, and not-for-profits. Some of the Cadbury ideas have become deeply ingrained: splitting the chairman and chief executive roles; strengthening the role of the audit committee through ensuring that only independent directors sit on it; insisting that independent directors have access to external legal advice paid for by the company; and clarifying the importance of ensuring the competence of both the chairman and company secretary. Cadbury has done much to restore the supremacy of the board's ultimate power and accountability, as well as its integrity.

This had a remarkably positive effect on boardroom behavior in the UK and Commonwealth, especially by re-establishing the proper independent powers of the chairman and the subsequent strengthening of the board roles of critical review, independent thought, and care-full decision-taking. These have been found very useful in improving board performance, rather than merely board conformance. Sadly, however, nothing is perfect and the Cadbury Committee kept, and even reinforced, the legally confusing distinction between executive directors and independent (nonexecutive) directors.

Other reports

The Cadbury Committee begat the Greenbury Committee *Director's Remuneration: Report of a Study Group* in 1995,[4] an unhappy and unsuccessful attempt to tackle the then heated argument on executive directors' pay and conditions. In turn this begat the Hampel Report, *Committee on Corporate Governance Final Report* in 1998,[5] which considered outstanding issues from the previous reports in more detail. These three reports were revised and published as *The Combined Code of the London Stock Exchange.*[6]

The UK has also pressed ahead with two very controversial reports and one even more highly controversial legislative proposal. It is beginning to move from mere board conformance toward a "board performance" approach. First, in 1999 the Turnbull Report, *Internal Control: Guidance for Directors on the Combined Code*[7] from the Institute of Chartered Accountants, argued that boards of listed companies must report to their shareholders annually on their risk-assessment and decision-making processes, or explain why not. This was received with such disbelief by so many boards that they had to scramble at the end of their first reporting year to explain to their shareholders why they had done little about it. In truth, many had not a clue what to do. The Turnbull Report assumed that the board undertook rigorous risk assessment and decision-taking around the boardroom table, whereas many boards often thought that was the executives' job. There is currently some angst in UK boardrooms as the implications of the Turnbull Report for board competence sink in.

Second, the Myners' Report of 2000[8] for the Insurance Industry Association brought back the original trigger concern of the mis-management of pension funds. Myners proposed that trustees of pension funds should be trained to competence, so that they deliver the necessary higher standards of statutory care and thereby can oversee their fund managers properly. It suggested also that they employ outside, more professional custodians. Even more controversially, it insisted that institutional investors *must* intervene in their under-performing investments. Again, this has caused great fluttering in the dovecotes of boards managing pension funds and the fund managers themselves. However much boards dislike Myners, its thinking is here to stay because while the public do not trust directors, they trust fund managers' competence even less. Myners offers the possibility of ensuring both accountability and competence.

Third comes the follow-on legislative proposal from the UK government that, given the Myners' Report and also continuing worries over the underperformance of private pension funds, trustees and fund managers *must* intervene in any badly run companies on their books. The pensions industry is implacably opposed to any more legislation; although given the lack of clarity in the UK pensions industry this might be one time when legislation would help. Since the UK government is also receiving three different pensions reviews—Sandler, Pickering, and the Inland Revenue—there is still time for a very British self-regulatory compromise to be thrashed out.

In early 2003 the Higgs Review of the role of nonexecutive directors will be published. The draft Higgs Report recommends:

❖ At least half a board, including the chairman, should be independent directors. A chief executive should not become chairman of the same company.

❖ A senior independent director should champion the interests of the shareholders and act as their intermediary with the executives.

❖ Prospective independent directors must undertake due diligence on the company to ensure that they have the knowledge, skills, experience, and time to make a constructive contribution. A company nomination committee should review the performance of independent directors.

❖ Independent directors' pay should be made up of an annual director's fee, an attendance fee, and additional fees if they chair company committees. Independent directors should not hold share options in their companies.

❖ The independent directors must meet at least once a year without the chairman or executive directors.

❖ The pool of candidates for independent directorships should be broadened and an independent director should usually serve for no more than two terms.

❖ A full-time executive director should have no more than one independent director role, and should not be chairman of another FTSE 100 company. No one should be chairman of more than one FTSE 100 company.

❖ Companies should indemnify independent directors against legal action, and ensure appropriate insurance cover.

❖ The Higgs Report should be incorporated into the UK best practice code on corporate governance. The Financial Reporting Council, and government, should review the impact of the report after two years.

Best practices in corporate governance

Following Cadbury, many countries have joined in the generation of codes of corporate governance and best practices. Indeed, it has become something of a cottage industry. The two I would refer you to as the most broadminded and advanced are the King Commission (1995 and 2002)[9] in South Africa, which is unique as it consciously sets out to integrate corporate governance with racial and social equality; and the Commonwealth Association for Corporate Governance Guidelines (1997),[10] which are distinctive in being derived multinationally from practitioners on all six continents. They are being implemented at varying speeds by the Commonwealth countries following agreement from all their heads of government. In addition, it is noteworthy that currently the US, Singapore, Hong Kong, China, Japan, Australia, New Zealand, Germany, and Canada are responding to growing public criticism of weak corporate governance practices.

Why should they worry? Mainly because internationally investors are becoming much more choosy about where they put their money, especially in a recession. The complex pressures driving corporate governance reform internationally are beginning to show that directing is a proper job, a complex job, and an intellectually demanding job, which requires much time to be spent on thinking strategically, reviewing, and deciding. Directing is now seen increasingly as a profession set in a global context, and competent directing as crucial to the development of liberal democracies.

Seven External Pressures for Improving Board Performance

I wish directors had to sit a PPE—Philosophy, Politics, and Economics—examination before being given a "license to direct." This sums up for me the areas in which most directors desperately need educating to be able to cope with the complex and dynamic external demands on their business. Lack of knowledge is a major cause of boards' strategic incompetence, but how many directors do you know who even read and digest a newspaper seriously each morning as the key start to their day? It takes time to change both the mindset and behavior of a board so that its members become comfortable with their strategic roles and tasks and with regular and open review of their performance.

The growing and complex pressures for improving board performance will not go away. Indeed, they are likely to grow rapidly. This is not surprising given the growing list of disquieted "stakeholders" involved:

- ❖ The public and politicians.
- ❖ Shareholders.
- ❖ Pressure groups.
- ❖ Listing directors.
- ❖ Liability insurers.
- ❖ Auditors.
- ❖ Potential and existing directors.

The very complexity of the possible permutations within this list for any board to have to consider gives an idea of the desperate need for treating directing as a profession, at least among future directors. Finding the level of appropriate transparency for these parties is going to be a big issue for boards in the future.

Given the seven main players for more effective corporate governance listed above, there is a definite pattern emerging. The three values of effective governance—accountability, probity, and openness—are being demanded simultaneously from increasingly complex groupings of disenchanted stakeholders. While the term "stakeholder" can include the shareholders, it usually refers to those people who do not have legal ownership of the business but have both emotional ownership and access to legal processes to constrain the board. So staff members, trade unions, suppliers, NGOs, local communities, and protectors of the physical environment all become stakeholders. Let us look in more detail at these seven pressure groups.

Public and Political Disquiet

This is an area where the governance of countries and corporate governance of companies are beginning to overlap. The realms of politicians, business, and public administration often have fuzzy edges.

Unless there are clear guidelines and strong sanctions at both govern-ment and corporate levels, it is only too easy for what seems at the time reasonable political expedience among power players to be seen later as sleaze or downright corruption by investors and the public. This was not such a visible issue in western democracies while the financial strings were pulled by governments, big business, and the trade unions. This triad of powers worked on the well-proven assumption that provided the general public were kept in the dark, they would be grateful for what fell off the bargaining table. However, growing public economic, financial, and political literacy, combined with better global communication systems and an awareness of the need for more scrutiny of the values and performance of the power players, are leading to a sea-change in the public's expectations of board values and processes.

Boards of directors in western democracies, and to an extent in the East Asian "Tiger economies," are becoming more aware of two uncomfortable facts. First, their personal liability is now open to increasingly close scrutiny by the owners of the business and so their personal and family wealth is on the line in a way it never has been before. If the company's shares and bonds are traded on the national and international financial markets, or are linked to the banks and governments that back them, then that scrutiny will increase. Second, the public still has little ability to assess company and board performance accurately or in any meaningful fashion. There is as yet no agreed International Accounting Standard. This way international political and social instability lies, because without transparency of market information to allow the free flow of investment, the capital-ist system is in trouble.

If people's wealth feels increasingly at the whims of unelected, incompetent, and irresponsible directors, then shareholders and stakeholders will resort either to law or finally to violence. As I write the Argentinian economy is collapsing and the Brazilian wobbling, due to political and corporate incompetence and general grasping political short-sightedness. The rising street violence in those coun-tries looks ominous. The vast majority of the issues leading to this dire state are self-induced: a lack of strategic awareness, a mixture of political and moral turpitude and corruption, plus the willingness of the masses to be seduced by such people through unsustainable bribes via unbacked government spending, especially on the public sector.

Even in the more stable but still volatile West such things happen. Political opportunism leads to corporate instability. Germany lost its solid deutschmark through Helmut Kohl's rash and emotional decision, on the reunification of the two Germanys, to exchange the weak East German mark at parity with the strong West German mark, and then to join the euro. The consequences have damaged Germany's economic performance profoundly, moving it within a decade from the strong man to the sick man of Europe. And that is before the demographic consequences of the over-generous but not fully funded public pension and social security plans hit home; and before even the medium-term consequences of joining the Eurozone are known.

This type of national government directoral incompetence and short-termism is highly worrying for the average western citizen. As they become much more financially aware and begin to ask questions about the competence of the boards of the companies in which their wealth is invested, they will become even more worried. For example, in the UK many "working-class" citizens living in public housing have accumulated wealth to pass on to their next generation. This was unthinkable even 40 years ago but now many are holding a pension, life assurance, and some shares from privatization. They are coming to notice, but possibly do not yet have the economic language to be able to express their anger at, political decisions eroding their wealth. As this has coincided with a global recession the rate of the erosion is seen to be increasing—as is the public's anger with, and distrust of, its political leaders. Some of this anger is now being directed increasingly at the behavior of corporate leaders.

The Marconi mess
In the UK there have been two recent high-profile scandals, Marconi and Equitable Life Assurance, both of which suggest strategic incompetence on the part of the boards rather than fraud or corruption. Both had been seen for years as rock-solid, dependable companies. Marconi plc was formed in 1999 from the communications and IT businesses

of the General Electric Company (GEC). Over 33 years under its redoubtable leader the late Lord Weinstock, GEC had built up a solid if unexciting reputation for producing high-quality electrical, engineering, telecommunications, and defense products, for creating shareholder value, and for being "mean," in that it had generated a cash pile of some £2.3 billion and was notoriously careful where it spent it. This was its cardinal sin according to the vested interests of the investment bankers, their brokers, and analysts. The reason Lord Weinstock gave for not investing more was that the projects around did not make good business sense and would not clear the hurdle of his high investment criteria—they would not add shareholder value.

Lord Weinstock's retirement led, with his agreement, to the recruitment of Lord Simpson of Dunkeld as managing director and John Mayo as finance director. Both had reputations in the City for being much more imaginative and were seen as "deal-makers"—to the unfettered delight of the investment bankers, whose "turns" would be considerable. Most shareholders had not expected the next two years to lead so rapidly to the destruction of the business. The sale of any non-telecoms-related businesses, the spending of the carefully garnered war chest, the plunge into massive debt, and an apparent strategy of bet-the-business on one industry—highly fashionable telecommunications—was the company's primrose path to everlasting corporate damnation. Remember that this was the period leading up to the "dot-com boom." Instead of realizing that the frenzy of greed and fear of losing out—which led to a seemingly collective agreement in the international business world to suspend the basic laws of economics—was fundamentally misplaced, the Marconi board proceeded to make high-cost acquisitions, buying at the top of the market. Lord Simpson was quoted in the *Sunday Times* as saying: "I spent the cash as fast as I could."

With commentators, entrepreneurs, and investors on both sides of the Atlantic chanting the unquestioned mantra "in future there will be no such thing as dividends; no such thing as profits; no such thing as cashflow; and the creation of future wealth will be solely dependent of the rise and rise of equity values," Marconi was set for a spectacular crash if anything went wrong with the telecoms industry. In a democracy with transparent communications no one can suspend the laws of economics for more than a few months, despite the huge wave of international cash that fueled this nonsense. And the inevitable happened—very quickly. The top three men had no experience of the volatile telecommunications industry. About £4 billion was wasted on two major acquisitions in the US.

When the dotcoms suddenly became dotbombs as financial reality began to re-establish itself, Marconi was left high and dry. Buying at the top of a market is never a wise strategy, neither is trying to sell at the bottom—but that is what Marconi did. As the whole technology, media, and telecommunications sector imploded internationally, it was completely wrong-footed. John Mayo and Lord Simpson left rapidly and without apology. From a market capitalization at its height of £34.5 billion Marconi was valued in August 2002 at £100.5 million. The share price crashed from some £12.50 to 0.15 pence in September 2002. The company is now struggling for rescue through rescheduling its debts. It looks as though the shareholders will receive about one penny per share. This was described in the *Sunday Times* with masterly understatement as a "very substantial dilution of equity value."

The shareholders and pensioners are furious and the key question they are asking is: "Where was the board?" The directors are meant to be the ultimate back-stop to protect the owners' interests, and yet, from what little is known publicly, they seem not to have fulfilled their fiduciary duty through rigorous critical review, risk assessment, and sound judgment. The board comprised a seemingly impressive list of City greats: Sir Alan Rudge, former deputy CEO of BT, Raymond Seitz, former US Ambassador to London, Nigel Stapleton, Chairman of Uniq dairy group, Sir William Castell, CEO of Americium medical group (who did voice concerns about the finances), Baroness Dunn, deputy chairman of HSBC (who stepped down in April 2002 to avoid a declared conflict of interest with HSBC, a major lender), and the previous chairman, Sir Roger Hurn. The jury is still out on whether they simply went along for the ride and had no way of turning back; whether they were experienced board members but had insufficient diversity within that experience to know what was happening; whether they were duped; or whether they were merely incompetent.

Investigations by the Department of Trade and Industry should help unravel a sorry saga that has done much to damage the public image of directors in listed companies generally, but unlike in the US there is not likely to be an official public inquiry.

Matters have been made worse in the public's mind by, for example, the behavior of the board of directors of Equitable Life Assurance. In essence, some ten years ago the board took a strategic decision to guarantee the future pension levels of one category of investors at the apparent expense of other investors. Precisely how the obvious risks were assessed, what the role of the actuaries was, and what the board questioning and risk-assessment processes were at that time will be brought out in the government inquiry. But again, the board took an unwise decision that also "bet the company"—a company of seemingly great probity and longevity, which handles the pensions of many of the UK's vocal middle classes, including politicians. As they see their accumulated wealth eroding they are exceedingly angry, and are looking for restitution and revenge. Where was the board?

Again, the board seemed to be a mixture of the great and the good, including Peter Sedgwick, chairman of Schroders, Jenny Page of the Millennium Dome and Railtrack, Peter Davis, ex-National Lottery Regulator, and three previous Equitable managing directors, Christopher Headdon, Roy Ranson, and Alan Nash. Were they objectively reviewing the risk assessments and decision-taking processes proposed by their executives? Or were they seduced by the complexity of actuarial and financial technobabble, possibly reinforced by some smugness and an overly optimistic view of how the world would develop? Yet it is these types of policy and strategy issues on which a board, not the executives, must ultimately decide. It is worth noting again that both the Marconi and Equitable Life examples are not of corporate fraud, but of a failure to be able to assess strategic risks, take wise judgments, and implement business strategies effectively.

There is an ironic twist in the Equitable Life case that may well point an uncomfortable way ahead for all directors—the ex-directors are being sued by the new board. And their directors' and officers' liability insurance cover is being disputed by Royal & Sun Alliance on the grounds that their alleged failure of judgment over the treatment of insurance contracts falls outside the terms of the £5 million policy. The dispute has gone to arbitration, but the ex-directors are complaining that they should not be pursued as they face the threat of financial ruin despite having behaved honestly and having followed the advice of their own advisers. Should this case reach the courts it will be a defining moment for directors' liability.

In the US, France, Germany, Australia, and many other countries there are recent cases of inadequate boards failing in their fiduciary duty and their duty of care and competence. Enron's filing for bankruptcy has been seen as "corporate America's Watergate" and sent political, social, and economic shudders around the world's stock markets. The Enron board seems to have played little role in critically questioning the balance of strategic entrepreneurial drive with prudent control mechanisms, to the extent that former chairman and CEO Ken Lay and others are being charged with corporate fraud.

The control mechanisms seem to have been very weak indeed, as the charge is that some $600 million excess costs were hidden off the balance sheet, thereby dramatically increasing the company's profits and share price. If this is true, it is fraudulent. It is deliberately lying to the owners and regulators. Did the board know this? And what role did the audit committee, supposedly the key internal financial policeman led by Lord Wakeham, play? It is now for the judiciary, regulators, and legislators to decide.

To make matters worse, Enron's auditors, Andersen, were found guilty of obstruction of justice in that they deliberately destroyed the audit paperwork, thereby demolishing their own reputation and their global practice. The top Enron executives are now facing a criminal investigation for allegedly selling their shares just before the crash; Ken Lay is reported to have made some $123 million from so doing. Yet the crash wiped out the pension schemes of employees, with long-term employees suffering the worst through their 401k schemes. What were the board's values and priorities?

There is now a hunt in the US to find who else has been using such debatable accounting practices, with the inevitable dramatic weakening of stock prices and great areas of corporate uncertainty. Perhaps one should carry in the back of one's mind Mohandas K Gandhi's wise words:

It is difficult but not impossible to conduct strictly honest business. What is true is that honesty is incompatible with the amassing of a large fortune.

Investment guru Leon Levy, in his 2003 book *The Mind of Wall Street*,[11] makes the fundamental point that "the simple rhythm of markets is as predictable as human avarice ... Good times breed laxity, laxity breeds unreliable numbers, and ultimately unreliable numbers bring about bad times." It is the politicians' and regulators' role to stop laxity being bred.

The aftermath of the World Trade Center tragedy in September 2001 brought home to people that the world's financial systems are as useful to terrorists as to anyone else. That is the nature of open, real-time systems. The stock market is now highly likely to be turned into the next battleground for the US's war on terror and boards will be in the front line. Is it possible to put some filters in place without stopping the flow of constructive capital around the world? This is a massive problem with no easy solutions.

Shareholder Pressure

The above examples are merely a tiny sample of current corporate governance issues. Nevertheless, they alone have been sufficient to trigger a growing abreaction against board ignorance and incompetence, especially among shareholders.

Direct and indirect shareholding is growing across the western world and increasingly in the developing world. Two-thirds of US foreign direct investment is in Argentina, Brazil, China, Russia, South Korea, and Mexico. The huge majority of US equity capital flow is into Hong Kong, Singapore, Taiwan, and South Korea, all of which are in surplus, so do they actually need the capital? Investing is as much an emotional issue as a rational one; otherwise who would touch China, for example? Many do, but most shareholders expect cool, rational, risk-assessed, and openly declared board decisions. This poses a true dilemma for directors; I will deal with the emotional aspects of board decisions in the next chapter.

Investors are learning to become much more careful in protecting their personal wealth. Leaving it entirely in the hands of, for example, financial advisers, fund managers, and pension fund trustees, and reviewing the situation once a year, is at best foolish in turbulent markets. The pressure by the owners for real-time shareholder transparency is growing rapidly and boards must respond to it.

Real-time transparency comes about mainly through investors' desire to see immediately how their investments are performing—the internet works wonderfully for this—and to have the option of building or reducing that investment if it is in their interest. Technology is helping here and investment companies such as Fidelity allow investors to see how their investments are performing in real time, even if in the current economic climate such information may be bleak.

This is having two effects. First, it is rapidly increasing the education of those indirect investors who use fund managers for their pension schemes or unit trusts. These "ordinary" investors are also voters. As they become more financially aware they are asking more informed questions of their fund managers and politicians. League tables of fund manager performance are becoming more easily available, and so the pressure grows. This, in turn, means that the selection by the fund manager of shares with undiscovered potential is increasingly a more competitive and subtle process. Consequently, fund managers are becoming much more questioning and inclined to want to audit the board composition, processes, and performance of the companies in which they invest. If proposed UK legislation goes through, for example, fund managers will have a duty to intervene in under-performing companies. Many boards—and fund managers—are simply not prepared for this. When first questioned rigorously on their present and likely future performance, boards can become resentful and aggressive, often because they are unsure themselves.

Such fund manager pressure will not go away. Indeed, it will increase, as shown by the following letter from the *Financial Times* by Tony Watson of the respected activists Hermes Pensions Management[12]:

Boards Must Communicate Strategy Better

Sir, In his admirable article "Time to listen to the shareholders" (January 22, 2002) Peter Martin raises crucial questions, not just for the investment industry but for the management of the economy. For generations the response of shareholders to under-performing companies has been to take the Wall Street Walk and sell the shares. Warren Buffett calls it "gin rummy capitalism"; discard your worst card at every turn. The result is that for extended periods companies under-perform and shareholders do little about it.

At Hermes we take the attitude that we are the agents of the owners of companies and that assets which have good owners will, in the long run, be more valuable than those without. Our belief is resolute in the fiduciary and stewardship obligations that we owe to our clients and which we believe the boards of our investee companies owe to us and them. Any dialogue to help all parties with these obligations is best conducted out of the public gaze, and, through the shareholding voting process, we are bound by the democratic result. We are committed to the belief that it is the job of the board and management to run the company. It is not ours. But there are going to be occasions when issues of such strategic significance arise that we would be derelict in our duty if we did not exercise our judgement and intervene.

However, to take issue with Mr Martin, it is a mistake to believe that there would be a bias towards caution. We are unaware of any hard evidence to support his contention. Equity investment is risky. We and our clients know that. We also know that from time to time things will go wrong. As investors, we have no conflict of interest by joining with the board to try to avoid them. We will always support well argued strategy, particularly if backed by past success.

We have now reached a point in the corporate governance debate where both managements and investors must recognise the obligation to find better ways in which strategy is communicated, understood and supported by all involved. In so doing the relationship between these groups will be strengthened. We must not allow it to deteriorate into the adversarial. While managements may have a wider agenda as Mr Martin suggests, to believe that their objective should be to achieve anything other than enhanced shareholder value over the longer term is to confuse means with ends. The interests of shareholders and boards are common. Boards can rely on our support but they must help us to support them in our joint enterprise.

In the US the California Public Employee Retirement System (CalPERS) is taking an equally tough stance. It is the largest public employees' pension fund in the world and has adopted a consistently advanced line on where its owners' funds will be invested. In the late 1990s it broke from its exclusively US base and started serious investment abroad, setting up a London office and talking of a Frankfurt one. Like Hermes and LENS, CalPERS has taken a consistently ethical and medium-to-long-term (around seven years is the average shareholding) perspective with its investments. Its criteria for share selection include, for example, country stability, the establishment of the basis of democracy, political risk, company liquidity, quality of financial controls, quality of national accounting standards (especially transparency criteria), quality of stock exchange regulation, and quality of national corporate governance systems. CalPERS is now giving equal weighting to issues such as labor regulation as well as market regulation.

In early 2002 it made the controversial decision to pull out of investing in public equities in Indonesia, Malaysia, Thailand, and the Philippines—all of which outperformed world markets in 2001—having already removed itself from Russia and China although, curiously, not Turkey or Argentina. This sent a shudder through already economically weakened emerging capital markets. The reasons given by CalPERS were that these countries continually failed a mixture of the above criteria, but with the Philippines criticized particularly on financial grounds, and Indonesia and Malaysia on social grounds.

The action enraged emerging markets in their desperate need for capital, even though only six emerging equity markets are seen to have sufficient liquidity to sustain "proper" investment. However, CalPERs will begin to invest in Poland and Hungary and will continue with Argentina, Brazil, the Czech Republic, Israel, Mexico, Peru,

South Africa, South Korea, Taiwan, and Turkey. This now creates the basis for a global experiment as to whether "socially responsible investing" (SRI) will work in the medium and long term.

Two further shareholder pressures will be added to make a board's life more demanding in future. First, individual investors are becoming more computer literate and use the internet as a real-time source of information on company performance. As many of them are active, intelligent, articulate, and retired—"gray surfers"—they have time to take the activity seriously enough to be able to give chairmen and boards a hard time. This is especially true at annual general meetings, to which they can turn up *en masse*, informed, and with plenty of proxy votes in their back pockets—a combination to worry any chairman. They often form clubs or interest groups who chat online frequently about their investment's performance. This can be unnerving for some boards who are used to unfettered decision-making power bestowed by the obscurity of their board processes and accounting procedures.

Matters are made worse for boards by the arrival of websites belonging to active interest groups determined to change company policies for their own ends, who are willing to publish highly contentious material to achieve their objectives. Some are well-known NGOs: Greenpeace, Friends of the Earth, World Wildlife Fund, Oxfam, etc. Others are more specific interest sites that are anti-company for whatever reason—disenchanted shareholders or staff, or "whistleblowers" (backed increasingly by legislation)—such as IBMsucks, or SaneBP, and others too vulgarly named to mention here. Their main aim is to fight a propaganda war with the corporation to achieve their campaigning ends, with their main weapon being bad publicity used against the corporation. Nevertheless, such action can backfire dramatically, as Greenpeace found over the *Brent Spar* affair with Shell. The immediate aim of such sites and shareholder pressure groups is to gather enough proxy votes to swing votes at an annual or extraordinary general meeting and so change board policies. Boards must learn to be prepared for them and such training is well outside executive roles.

The final pressure for increasing board awareness of shareholder demands comes from the "shadow side" of what can otherwise be seen as a welcome opening up to the owners and stakeholders of the underlying values behind board risk-assessment and decision-taking processes. By far the worst example is the pillorying of research company Huntingdon Life Sciences and the sustained attempt to force it out of business by protestors against animal experimentation. After buying some shares to get access to basic company information, including directors' home addresses, there are two main tactics: direct physical confrontation with board members and employees of the company, and cutting off its funds by active intimidation of the funders. No matter how heartfelt the values of the protestors, much of the intimidation is illegal and increasingly uses terrorist tactics. This is raising major questions for boards over how to handle their future policies and strategies, particularly the areas in which they will invest for the future, and whether the law will protect them if they stay within it.

Pressure Group Disquiet

The rise of outspoken and demanding pressure groups is a phenomenon of the late twentieth century. As the undeniable differences between rich and poor across the world are made more manifest, so increasing demands for accountability, honesty, and transparency are made on boards and individual directors by these pressure groups. Their main aims are to rock or destroy the reputation of the corporation and so wreck its share price, trigger shareholder discontent, and get rid of the board and its policies.

The big players in these newish fundraising and campaigning fields are such nongovernmental organizations (NGOs) as the Red Cross, Red Crescent, Greenpeace International, Amnesty International, Médicins sans Frontières, World Wildlife Fund, etc. They are beginning to learn that head-on confrontation is rarely successful in the long term and so are striking some fragile cooperation deals with their targets. However, there are thousands of smaller charities spread around the world and it these that cause many boards growing concern as to their political ends and funding methods. There is no doubt

that the vast majority do good. They raise great public hope on specific issues and are usually creatively skilled at getting free media cov-
erage. Teamed up with local groups well-informed about specific
interests they can be very effective, especially if they can get an ill-
informed, or just plain obnoxious, executive from the offending company in front of the cameras. While big players like the Red Cross take
a hard line on presenting a nonpolitical stance, others can be seen as
decidedly the opposite.

Irene Kahn is Secretary General of Amnesty International, working
with a budget of some £25 million and a staff of 355 paid employees
and 91 volunteers. She is fighting to protect human rights at a time
when she feels that many governments are willing to trade these for
improved national security. Unlike environmental pollution and
workers' rights, it is not a very fashionable cause and unlikely yet to
raise interest in many boardrooms. She says in an interview in the
Financial Times[13]:

> *We see business as having human rights responsibilities, both within
> their own operations and in the influence they may have over gov-
> ernments and others. Some NGOs question why Amnesty is in the
> UN Global Compact, because the compact does not hold companies
> accountable. We believe we should try whatever way is possible to
> increase the pressure on corporations to respect human rights.*
>
> *We are having big discussions with our internal business
> groups on how we set benchmarks for our participation in these ini-
> tiatives. The big question is: when do you move from a promotional,
> friendly relationship with a company to an oppositional relation-
> ship? If things don't improve on the ground, then you have to take a
> tough stand and be open about it. When we name names we have to
> be absolutely sure of our information.*

Here speaks the voice of a reasonable but determined pressure group.
Such groups will not go away and they will undoubtedly influence
boardroom behavior in future.

However, others are not so well intentioned or organized. The
loose coalition going under the title of the Anti-Globalization Alliance

is at the opposite end of the spectrum, with an avowed aim of ending capitalism and redistributing wealth more fairly around the world. Its *bêtes noires* are the World Bank, the World Trade Organization, the International Monetary Fund, and especially the US Government.

Whatever your personal views, pressure groups have to be taken into a board's risk assessment calculations and will eat up a growing amount of board time. This is particularly true as "reputational risk" becomes such a big issue. The fear of many boards is that one big mistake will lead to long-term trouble in terms of diminution of shareholder value, the loss of most of their customers, or even the end of the business. So the notion of *corporate social responsibility* has grown rapidly and is being taken very seriously among more far-sighted boards. It is no coincidence that since its well-publicized problems with *Brent Spar* and Ogoniland, Shell has pioneered the idea of *triple bottom line* annual reporting to help rebuild its reputation, maintain its profits, and reinforce its future license to operate. The triple bottom line approach has three separate, minimum annual, audits of financial, physical environmental, and corporate social responsibility published to the shareholders and made easily available to the public.

A further problem for boards is that there are so many, and growing, legal or aspirational "rights"—human, animal, employment, maternity, disability, pension, environmental, local community, and medical, to name but a few—that a board has to be much better aware, informed, and capable of many more tough risk-assessment processes and resource-allocation decisions than before. However, it may be tempted to try to avoid the whole thing and hope that it will go away. During a recession such pressures may reduce in the short term, but in the West people increasingly want to see that their wealth is put into ethical investments that still generate a return. The two are not incompatible, and boards will have to show to more discerning shareholders precisely how they do this.

However, the NGOs are not shining beacons of the very practices for which they criticize others. Many "rights" groups have very debatable corporate governance practices of their own. These usually occur at two levels. Many do not subscribe to the notion that there is a reciprocal "duty" or duties for each "right." Many believe that on occasion it is OK to break the law because the end justifies the means. This is the claim of single-interest campaigners down the centuries, whether terrorists, religious fundamentalists, political activists, or just plain criminals. Sometimes it works and they come to power. But history shows us that they then revert to the very values and behavior against which they had originally campaigned.

The corporate governance of NGOs is a hot topic at present. I have worked with some of them on this very issue and have come away disappointed by their innate conservatism and short-sighted need to keep a firm grip on the levers of existing organizational power. While the public gives big money to many of these organizations, the distribution of such funds fairly around the impoverished parts of their own organization is often not so obvious. Donors are not treated as either owners or active members of the organization with their own rights. Often there are no democratic procedures internally for deciding who has what power, for how long, and how their performance is to be measured. The corporate governance values of accountability, probity, and transparency are not yet well developed in many NGOs—but need to be if they are to maintain their own long-term reputations.

Listing Director Disquiet

The listing director of a stock exchange is responsible for stating the conditions under which a stock can be listed and quoted on that exchange.

When ownership of shares and trading in them was closely held to a very small group of wealthy people with their own social sanctions on miscreants, there was no great need to police the listing of shares and the subsequent behavior of boards and directors. However, as we move into an era of much wider share ownership and less sophisticated and less powerful investors, greater public scrutiny and better sanctions are needed both at the listing stage and later in monitoring the corporate governance of listed companies.

Hence the flexing of muscles by listings directors around the world. And I do mean around the world. In the chase after international capital flows it is now necessary for countries, through their stock exchanges, to offer much greater certainty to potential investors about the three basic values of corporate governance: accountability, probity, and transparency. In many countries it is no longer mandatory to list on your own stock exchange. So if you want to list on London or New York, Frankfurt, Paris, Hong Kong, Sydney, Singapore, Mauritius, or even Shanghai it is easy—provided that you stick by the listings rules. Listing is becoming an internationally competitive business and listing directors are competing both on price and by ensuring investors better certainty through effective corporate governance standards and accounting transparency.

There is a tightening of local accounting rules and a move away from the relatively lax US-GAAP standards toward developing an accepted International Accounting Standard; moves to counter corruption and terrorism, especially money laundering; the wider acceptance of an anti-corruption standard like the US Foreign Corrupt Practices Act, which makes it a crime for a US citizen to bribe a official overseas; and much greater openness in the presentation of business information to the owners, including the risk-assessment and decision-making processes of the board.

Typical of the toughening demands are a set of proposals published by the Hong Kong Stock Exchange in January 2002. The three main headings of the proposed amendments to the Hong Kong Listing Rules characterize the main issues facing listings directors. I have selected some of the main proposals:

Protection of shareholder rights

❖ Voting by poll for connected transactions and all resolutions requiring independent shareholders' agreement.

❖ Issuers to satisfy the Exchange that they are in severe financial difficulties or other exceptional circumstances if they wish to issue shares under a general mandate and the price represents a discount of 20 percent or more of the benchmarked price set out in the consultation paper.

Directors and board practices

❖ Issuers to appoint independent nonexecutive directors representing no less than one-third of the members of their boards and not fewer than two in any event.

❖ Minimum standard of board practices to be set out in the code of best practice that the Exchange would recommend all issuers to meet.

❖ Issuers to include a report on corporate governance practices in annual reports.

❖ The establishment of an audit committee to be made mandatory.

Corporate reporting and disclosure

❖ Main board issuers to publish quarterly reports and issue quarterly results within 45 days after the quarter end.

Life will become much tougher and more rigorous nationally and internationally for listed companies in the immediate future on these dimensions. Any company thinking of an initial public offering (IPO) will, after the dotbombs, have a much more rigorous set of criteria to meet before listing even on a junior exchange. While this should help reduce some uncertainties it will not, and cannot, reduce the essence of business—the taking of capital risk.

That makes it doubly troubling that a draft EU Directive seeks to erode the international "gold standard" of UK listing rules and reduce them to a one-size-fits-all European mediocrity in a bid to create a "single passport" for all new issues. The UK's biggest shareholders are very concerned that standards will be weakened at the very time when they should be tightened. If this happens, the fear is that investor protection will be weakened and shareholders will not be able to exercise their responsibilities properly. For example, under the EU proposals companies may have to disclose market-sensitive data only in quarterly reports, not in real time, thereby destroying investor comfort.

Directors' and Officers' Liability Insurers

It is a sad sign of our times that we are becoming a more litigious society. Whereas many countries have seen the US as over-litigious and prone to rush to the law on the most minor of matters, we are now all moving down that slippery slope. Increasing litigation can be seen as an obvious consequence of directors' lack of training and subsequent lack of fiduciary duty and care, particularly when this comes under scrutiny from a wider share ownership of increasingly wary investors who have access both to much better-quality information about business and to lawyers willing to work on a "no win, no fee" basis.

The increasing tendency of investors, employees, customers, third parties, and suppliers to sue and the recent corporate scandals are having a devastating effect on companies' insurance rates, especially for directors' and officers' liability insurance.

An article by Adrian Michaels in the Financial Times explains[14]:

A senior executive of AIG, the world's largest insurer, ... warned that following the Enron scandal the insurance industry was facing a disastrous run of claims over policies that cover shareholder lawsuit liabilities. Thomas Tizzio, senior vice-chairman at AIG, said that the financial fall-out from the energy trader's collapse and other high-profile failures, such as the recent bankruptcy filing of retailer K-Mart, were a "wake-up" call for the insurance industry.

Insurers write "Directors and Officers" (D&O) policies for companies that are triggered when shareholders file lawsuits after financial shocks. As well as covering rewards, insurers are usually obligated to pay legal fees and these account for the lion's share of their liabilities, even if the companies eventually defeat the suits. Mr Tizzio, commenting on the severe market jitters over corporate accounting in recent weeks, said insurers needed to understand the companies they covered and the risks to which they were committing themselves. Over 50 lawsuits have been filed against Enron's directors and executives, seeking compensation and alleging that shareholders were not given an accurate financial picture of the company. Mr Tizzio implied that insurers had not charged nearly enough for D&O premiums in general. "The focus in 2002 will be on D&O in corporate America," he said. "This year could ultimately see a catastrophic loss in that sector."

The Insurance Information Institute believes that D&O will be the largest liability problem for the industry this year, even as it battles uncertainty over claims from future terrorist attacks. It is estimated that US$3bn in D&O premiums was taken in the last year but that insurers may have to pay out more than $5bn. Mr Tizzio, in a rare public appearance ... said there had been 487 class action claims for securities fraud in federal courts last year. In 2001 that had been just 216. The number of suits started to grow dramatically with the bursting of the dotcom bubble and there is no end in sight.

According to Bob Hartwig of the Insurance Institute, "the premium rates that were charged did not anticipate the tremendous surge in suits." [After Enron] the entire investment community has had the revelation that audited accounts were not worth the paper they are written on.

Growing Auditor Disquiet

Do not be lulled into a false sense of security by the public outcry, and proposed changes, following questioning of the auditors' role after the Enron affair. However disgracefully some of them are proved to have behaved, auditors still carry out an onerous, necessary, and complex task—and, surprisingly, by so doing often allow the board off the hook. For example, in the UK and Commonwealth the auditors, not the directors, take the responsibility for stating publicly that the company's finances are "a true and accurate account" and so allow investors to conclude that they must be investing in a going concern. This is very curious, as logically it should be the directors who make this statement and are held personally and criminally liable for it, as is now the case in the US. If the proposed UK Company Law Review Bill is passed by Parliament, this will happen in the UK. It is already the law in South Africa.

Harvey Pitt, chairman of the US Securities and Exchange Commission, declared in June 2002 his backing for a new regulation that would force US CEOs and financial officers not only to sign all quarterly and annual financial disclosures made to the SEC as at present, but also to certify formally that the returns contain all important information about the company—a change Mr. Pitt called an "unassailable concept." He termed these proposals "historic—and long overdue." He went on, "The CEO should not be able to say, 'Gee, I wasn't aware!' or 'I'm flying at 50,000 feet and I did not know of certain disclosures.' The officers will be held to this standard and there will be criminal liability [of up to 20 years' jail] for any mis-statement or omission."

Auditors were beginning to toughen up their act before Enron. However, in the future they, and a company's officers, will have to show a level of inspectoral rigor that is not always manifest currently. For the four biggest international auditors matters have been muddied by all of them expanding out of boring, mechanical, and relatively low-paid auditing work and consequent tax and related advice into the exciting, sexy, and well-paid work of providing consultancy services. This has laid them open to the charges of frequent conflicts of interests, both by being lenient in their audit process because they hoped to get big consultancy fees, and of staying with a client much too long on consultancy assignments so that they were not sufficiently at arm's length for disinterested auditing work.

Even so there have been some honorable exceptions. The first ground tremor in the UK came when the then Coopers and Lybrand resigned from its audit of a computer games manufacturer because of "weak corporate governance systems." This was unheard of, but led to a growing number of qualified accounts, or resignations, as the importance of linking effective corporate governance and accounting systems has come to be appreciated by both auditors and shareholders.

Existing and Potential Director Disquiet

If the previous six external pressures for improving directoral competence all seem to directors to be a gross imposition on boards, the good news is that there is a growing number of existing directors who not only think that the future must embrace an assessment of board competence but have set out to do something about it. They accept the need for assessable competence as a given—the need for a "license to direct." For them the question is not "whether" or "when" but "How can we do it now?" They want directors to become professionals.

So far the signs are remarkably optimistic. For example, the Institute of Directors in London has developed accreditation for Chartered Director status awarded through the Privy Council.[15] The author must declare an interest in this as he has spent over five years helping launch this globally unique award, the details of which are given in Chapter 8.

However, even Chartered Director status cannot guarantee directoral competence. Competence comes from using a combination of appropriate knowledge, attitudes, and skills. The present IoD examination process does not attempt to assess skills in a specific situation, but it does guarantee both a certain level of assessed knowledge and attitudes, and five years of real directoral experience (not merely single functional experience) that mark Chartered Directors out from the rest. As Chartered Directors must sign a code of conduct and promise to maintain continuing professional development annually, it is a significant step toward the idea of creating a director's license to operate.

Although this development can be seen as a UK and Commonwealth phenomenon, that is not the case. Unexpectedly, the Japanese Management Association recently took the Chartered Director notion and created its own culturally adapted version, and this set a number of other countries in pursuit of the idea.

The combination of these seven external pressures is beginning to cause a growing number of shareholders and directors to see that their, and their board's, survival and growth will come by being able to convince a wider public that directoral competence can be created and used for their mutual benefit. This will be through the development of shareholder- and stakeholder-friendly board and director's knowledge, skills, and attitudes.

However, the vast majority of directors are not in this enlightened position and struggle on in ignorance and the vain hope that they will somehow not be found out. Such lack of accurate information leads to bluffing and then to major abuses of power around the boardroom table. It is to these that I wish to turn in the next two chapters.

CHAPTER THREE

Back to Basics

Reasserting the Superiority of the Board

D IRECTORS' IGNORANCE OF THEIR RIGHTS, duties, roles and tasks, combined with weak chairmanship, ensures abuse of the key corporate direction-giving process around the boardroom table. This leads inevitably to under-performance by both the board and the business.

One of the key problems in the abuse and misappropriation of board roles is misunderstanding the roles and tasks of the "chief executive." This very fashionable job title is usually a misnomer for managing director. I stress again that a chief executive is not a member of a board but reports to it. By definition, a managing director is a full board member. Using the wrong job title shows both a lack of legal knowledge of corporate governance and sloppy thinking by those making the appointment. This, in turn, has led to many global myths about the sources of power on a board of directors.

It is curious that the chief executive is seen as such an all-powerful figure in most organizations, private or public. Although they often act as if they own the enterprise, they do not. Indeed, one can argue strongly that most of the present US corporate governance problems are caused by this wrong assumption. At law CEOs have little absolute power—that resides in the board of directors and is exercised on behalf of the shareholders. Indeed, in UK, US, and Commonwealth law a chief executive is not a member of the board of directors unless he or she carries the formal title of "director" as well.

A true chief executive would report to a board, debate with it, take instructions from it, but not be a voting part of it. The very phrase itself tells you that this is the head of the executive function—the operational side of the organization—not of the board. Even the title "chairman" is rarely mentioned in most Companies

Acts, Insolvency Acts, or Ordinances, although it is a much more important role legally.

The proper title for the senior executive who is also a properly constituted board member is "managing director," but few people seem to care, until they end up on the wrong end of litigation. During this chapter and the rest of the book I shall try to be more rigorous and use managing director as the specific role, using the term chief executive only when referring to an existing job title.

Let us be truly radical and go back to the roots of company law as it evolved in the Anglo-Saxon world. The only job titles that have serious legal authority at board level, and consequent duties and liabilities, are "director" and "company secretary" (an officer of the board, but not a board member). I will deal with the latter later.

Directors are designed to be a group of equals who meet collegially around the boardroom table under the neutral guidance of the chairman, elected by them as *primus inter pares*, to agree the future direction of the business and ensure its prudent control. In this strict sense directors are never executives. The term "executive director" is a legal nonsense, as is "nonexecutive" or "independent director." A director is a director.

Directors should, therefore, be paid and treated equally. Because this is not understood by most directors or owners and, therefore, rarely acted on, the corrosive processes of board under-performance usually start here. This is particularly true if the board is dominated by executives who also have a director functional job title, e.g., finance director or marketing director, but who do not understand nor live out their proper directoral responsibilities. This statement will come as a shock to many existing directors, most of whom are still defined only by their legally nonexistent board titles including finance director, commercial director, and in the US chief financial officer, chief operating officer, president, vice-president, etc.

Indeed, many existing directors think that because they are protected by "limited liability" all these legal niceties are unimportant. That is not true either. Therefore they are often shocked to find that the limitation of liability is only on the paid-up share capital of the shareholders, not the directors. Most do not realize that directors have unlimited personal liability for their actions, or inactions, as well as corporate liability as a member of a board of directors. Moreover, of those who do know the law, most rationalize that they still do not need to worry much as they are covered by their directors' and officers' liability insurance policy. To a limited extent this may be so, but in a world becoming more litigious by the day, insurers are much more rigorous on checking that the board and individual directors exercise their directoral duties competently, especially those of care and trust. If the insurers can find a way of not paying, they will, and then the director's personal and family wealth is on the line.

Directors across the rich world now face much tougher future legislation regarding their responsibility in such areas as, for example, the pollution of the physical environment, breaking health and safety at work laws, corporate killing, and fraud. It is therefore clear to me that the collegiality and professionalism of boards must rise rapidly if we are to continue to have people wishing to take on the onerous liabilities of a company director, private or public. Who would want to be an incompetent director in the future?

Nevertheless, chief executives can do much to block the rise of professionalism and competence on boards, as we shall see in this chapter.

How Chief Executives Take Unlimited Power

Given many directors' lack of legal and practical knowledge, it is easy to see how we have reached the paradoxical position where the world of shareholders and stakeholders is demanding much higher levels of competence from directors, yet most organizations rely increasingly on a single, powerful chief executive to see them through. Such chief executives usually have the power to "bet the business" with very little critical review or thoughtful debate from their notional boardroom colleagues, let alone the shareholders.

There are four main reasons for this over-reliance on one powerful person:

❖ The ignorance of board roles, tasks, and liabilities on the part of
  most people who are selected to become directors.
❖ Many directors' willingness to go for a quiet life, usually at the end
  of a successful managerial or professional career, by not rocking the
  boat, and their consequent failure to fulfill their duty of asking
  probing questions of a powerful personality.
❖ A skewed public perception that the chief executive role is not
  merely important in itself but is symbolic of the deeper, cultural
  basis of capitalism.
❖ Shareholders', trustees', and the public's ignorance of the board's
  true roles and tasks.

Given these observations, it can be seen that not all chief executives
grab power greedily. Many just pick it up because it is lying there with
no one else willing to touch it.

Let us look at these four reasons in more detail.

Ignorance of Board and Directors' Roles and Tasks

In 1992 the Institute of Directors (IoD) in London surveyed its members and found that less than 8 percent of them had even one day's
training in being a director. This was an astonishing finding as, by definition, those who had sought IoD membership could be assumed to
be more likely than most to desire competence as a director. Later
checking internationally showed that in world terms 8 percent was a
high result, and even in 2001 the percentage had only moved toward
15 percent. Perhaps more surprising, given that result, is that the UK
is considered by many to be the world leader in director development.
This is a deeply worrying comment on the global condition of effective corporate governance.

What is even stranger is the seemingly general acceptance of an
untenable proposition: that those given the most important jobs in the
organization—directing its future so that of all of those employed by
or associated with it create wealth and employment for the owners
and their wider society—should have no training for them. Training

and development budgets tend to disappear well before board level is reached. We seem to rely excessively on an ill-defined and weakly assessed notion called "experience" to get by. Unfortunately, such experience is rarely directoral. It is usually managerial and professional, and so concerned with the day-to-day operations of a business—these are not directoral roles and there is a big difference between managing and directing an organization.

Many of the "independent" directors recruited to boards are merely executive directors from other boards. Few will ever have had directoral training and assessment. The best that can be said about these "executive" nonexecutive directors is that such a new role can provide a start in widening their experience, albeit in an unstructured way. But as many sit on each other's audit and remuneration committees, the chances of self-censorship are high. The implicit emotional contract is "Don't ask me difficult questions and I won't ask you them either." If director training exists at all in such companies, it is usually semi-legalistic in nature and very "compliance oriented" in that it focuses on a "tick box" approach and there is an in-built assumption that once all boxes are ticked no further action is needed.

Nothing could be further from the truth. Board conformance is necessary but not sufficient. However, much thinking on where sufficiency comes from is muddled. There is at present an over-reliance on nonexecutive directors to correct matters. Yet as Michael Grade said at the Institute of Directors' Convention in 2000:

> *Nonexecutive directors are like bidets—no one knows what they are for, but they definitely add a bit of class.*

Sufficiency comes from regularly assessing the more difficult and less explored area of board performance. This is where it gets personal.

The notions of consciously seeking to re-establish the supremacy of the board, of having development programs for board and individual director competence, and of having that competence appraised at least annually are usually met with incredulous stares. Yet board training and development are rarely concerned with learning the board performance areas of systematic policy formulation, strategic thinking, risk assessment, and decision-taking processes that so clearly differentiate *directing* from *managing*.

Normally no induction, inclusion, or competence building is offered to new—or existing—directors in the majority of companies. So the strong message from the selectors on appointing a director is: "Well done! Now turn up and shut up. You will pick it up as you go along. Don't argue with the existing power players." What kind of message does this give a new director in developing their confidence to fulfill their interrogative role?

I have listed below six simple questions that I use to get a benchmark of how basic a board's training has been:

1 If I have the word "director" on my business card but am not a member of the board of my organization, do I have the same liabilities as a board member?
2 If I am a director of a limited liability joint stock company, am I covered as far as my personal liabilities are concerned?
3 Do nonexecutive (independent) directors have fewer responsibilities than executive directors?
4 In a limited liability company, is the prime duty of a director and the board to the shareholders?
5 If you are advising and working with a board, either as a senior manager or as a consultant, do you avoid directoral liability?
6 Are directors of state-owned organizations, including agencies and parastatals, exempt from normal directoral responsibilities?

Most get the first five wrong (answers on page 77) and no one knows the answer to number six, as it has not been tested by the UK and Commonwealth courts, nor in the US. However, in the UK there are best-practice guidelines suggested by government, essentially following the Companies Acts. My colleagues on the AMED Director Development Network have worked up this quiz into something more comprehensive and you can find it, and the detailed answers, in *The Effective Director*.[1]

This lack of even the most basic directoral knowledge is a dire state of affairs that, if we are seeking international improvement in directoral competence, can only be rectified by more rigorous selection, training, coaching, and development processes, for both boards and individual directors.

This is a global problem. However, as one example of what is being done to counter it, in 2002 the UK government proposed the first serious shake-up in company law for over a century. Among the main proposals for reform are the following:

❖ Directors and executives who mislead auditors could face unlimited fines and two years in jail.
❖ The definition of the role of the board and directors should be built into the memorandum and articles of association document, which will itself be redrafted as the company constitution.
❖ The responsibilities of directors are to be clarified around the principle "that their primary role is to promote the success of the company for the benefit of the shareholders as a whole."
❖ Public corporations with a turnover of more than £50 million and private companies with a turnover of more than £500 million must publish an operating and financial review, covering the main factors underlying the company's performance.
❖ A new Standards Board will be created to oversee the detailed accounting, reporting, and disclosure rules.
❖ Companies and their directors convicted of flouting company law would be named on a central register.

If passed in their present form by Parliament, these should greatly help counter directors' ignorance of their roles and tasks and ensure that the public is better informed.

Willingness to Go for a Quiet Life

If directors are for the most part ignorant of their roles and tasks, it follows that in the interest of their own survival they are unlikely to make this known, even within the board. Admitting ignorance is so humiliating, especially for a top person. Such directors are much more likely to expend their energies in and around the board on not getting found out, blaming others, focusing and asking searching questions only on their previous discipline to the exclusion of all others, and avoiding any position where they are likely to be put in a potentially embarrassing spotlight.

Therefore, there is little chance of them adequately fulfilling their directoral duty of critical review and debate through asking discerning questions of the chairman, managing director, or fellow directors. By failing to discharge these duties individually and collegially, the policy-formulating, idea-generating, risk assessment, strategic thinking, and decision-taking tasks of the board are eroded. I go into the psychology of this in Chapter 5, but here deal with some practical aspects.

We can see why this happens, but we should not forgive it. Asking questions, especially of the managing director, is seen by many executive directors as a career-limiting option, especially if the person you are questioning is also your direct boss. Even nonexecutive directors asking constructively critical questions are often seen as presumptuous and time-wasting by all the executive directors, especially the managing director. So the erosion of board effectiveness continues until only one or two powerful people actually run the business. This may well be in their short-term interests, but the role of the board in sustaining long-term organizational health is undermined.

This negative behavior can be countered by a mixture of training, directoral appraisal, and especially building self-confidence and moral integrity among board members. I shall spend a great deal of Part II dealing with how to do this.

Seeing the Chief Executive as the Bastion of Capitalism

Given the two conditions above, it is hardly surprising that chief executives—or, more correctly, managing directors—come to dominate their boards. They may be no more competent than any other board member, but they are assumed by most, inside and outside the corporation, to have absolute competence and so are granted absolute power. Why should this be so? I think that there are four main reasons.

The first is that the continuing erosion of the board's role within and without the enterprise means that the only person with obvious power, and a convenient focus for all praise and blame, is the head of the organization's executive function—the chief executive or managing director. With weak directors and chairmen, criticizing the CEO or managing director is often viewed as beyond the remit of the board. Legally this is nonsense, but custom and practice have deluded many boards into believing that this is the norm—and that they can do nothing about it, regardless of their onerous personal liabilities.

The rise of the celebrity CEO has not helped matters. These people appear frequently on the front covers of glossy magazines and tend to be seduced into living out a filmstar lifestyle that, in turn, gives reflected celebrity to other board members. This is fine when the going is good, as Jack Welch experienced for many years. But when criticism finally emerges, usually after the CEO has left the company, the destruction of their business and personal reputational image can be quick and brutal. For example, the sudden resignations of Tyco International's chief executive, Dennis Kozlowski, and its general counsel, Mark Belnick, may suggest that personal funding and tax evasion charges will mark the start of a painful period for them. Greed is not always good, personally or corporately, and the anger of the Tyco shareholders as their share price drops and the creditors and credit agencies begin to make their demands will rise for many months to come.

Second, the erosion of the board's function has led automatically to the erosion of the chairman's role. If we return to basics, then the chairman is the "boss of the board" who is charged with steering it neutrally to the wisest collegial decisions that it can make about the balance of driving forward while ensuring prudent control. The chairman is *not* the boss of the company. Neither is the managing director or chief executive, who is only the boss of its daily operations. It is essential that the chairman and the board first define their "reserved powers," and then learn how work together with the managing director to balance the legislatively designed sharing of power and effectively resolve the inevitable directoral dilemmas through using the diverse ideas, information, and experience of all board members and their direct reports.

I stress again that in a properly functioning board the managing director or chief executive has no legally defined role and is a colleague among equals. It is only when a managing director is on the other side of the boardroom door that he or she becomes boss of the operations of the business. This is difficult for many managing directors to come to terms with. They see themselves as having been selected for an all-powerful job, and sometimes view the board contemptuously as a minor inconvenience in the pursuit of their personal aims. The saying "There is no more dangerous person to the long-term health of an organization than a sixtyish CEO with just two years to go and a pocketful of stock options" contains more than a germ of truth. In such a case they feel that short-termism is all—the share price must be ramped up regardless of whether this adds shareholder value. Yet the board is meant to be the critical counterweight to any of the CEO's short-term, personal goals.

The third reason is the tendency, especially in the US, to demean the role of the board. This has been copied internationally in both the private and public sectors and is now beginning to reap a terrible revenge from the general public. When traveling and researching in the US, most people I speak to see the board of directors as an amusing and useless anachronism. There is often much giggling about this and then two particular comments. First, that the "real" directors in this organization are only those with director in their job title, i.e., those one rung below vice-president, "so they don't count." If pressed, the vast majority of US respondents will go into an embarrassed chant and comment to the effect that "the board of directors is ten friends of the chief executive, a woman and a black." A quick scrutiny of the Fortune 500 boards reveals just how true this can be. This is a major indictment of the lack of sufficient diversity in US corporate life, the consequences of which affect in turn much of the rest of the world.

The fourth and main reason is the continuing reification by the media and the public of the chief executive role, rather than the board, as the bastion of capitalism. This is not a new phenomenon—such greats as Adam Smith and Abraham Lincoln were exercised by it—but it has recently been noticeably re-emphasized. Both in the UK under Margaret Thatcher and in the US under Presidents Reagan, George

Bush, and George W Bush the unfeeling, socially fragmenting, aspects of capitalism have been over-stressed politically, with the media continually echoing Gordon Gecko's mantra "greed is good." Even Chinese Premier Deng Xiao Ping got in on the act with "It does not matter what color the cat is as long as it catches the mice."

If we look back to the US immediately after the Great Crash, we find the publication of a seminal book by Adolf Berle and Gardiner Means called *The Modern Corporation and Private Property*.[2] The book is virtually unknown by the general public, but its main line of argument has become the bible of rampant capitalists and the bane of many corporate governance reformers. If you accept Berle and Means' argument, then you can justify any use of absolute power to maintain the position of the executives, particularly the chief executive, and the continuing fragmentation of the shareholders' interests—in the short term. Indeed, in some parts of the US any criticism of this notion can be seen as basically "un-American."

Nevertheless, the public, shareholders, and even some members of the business world are becoming less enamored of such a simplistic and divisive idea. A counterconcept is growing: that there needs to be sufficient diversity of thought and debate on a board to enable effective critical review, risk assessment, and decision-taking in which the managing director/CEO will participate but not dominate. This idea is taking hold at a time when public demands, especially from increasingly disillusioned shareholders and pensioners, for more transparency over board and company performance are coinciding with the development of cheap, global information systems. More and more shareholders and stakeholders are holding their own debates about a company over the internet.

In future, boards will not be able to be as secretive and insensitive to wider policy issues and shareholder needs. The old argument that "only profit and the shareholders are important" can be sustained when there is a small shareholder base and little public interest in how boards add value in relation to their company's impact on communities and the physical environment. However, this argument is eroded very quickly when the shareholders are also members, or representatives, of a much wider public and ask more discerning questions about

such matters as the accuracy of published accounts and the consequences for their equity and pension fund investments. Shareholders
are also much better informed and less fragmented because they are
able to talk to each other in real time on the internet. Life is going to
become much more rigorous for directors, especially when they are
facing public scrutiny of the quality of board decisions.

Many will not like it and will leave early. It is to be hoped that they
will be replaced by others who understand and respect the notion that
directing is becoming a profession for which one must undertake serious study and examination. They will be the ones who help restore the
supremacy of the board.

Shareholder and Public Ignorance of Board Roles and Tasks

I hope the above sections have made the case for reasserting the role
of the board and rebalancing the power of the chief executive.
However, progress will be slow unless shareholders and the general
public become insistent that this is done. The world recession, the
dotbomb fiasco, and the learning post-Enron will all help. In the rich
nations we are seeing for the first time "ordinary" citizens with wealth
to hand on to future generations. They are only mildly financially literate, but are increasingly angry at the obvious loss of their wealth in
pensions, life policies, and investments since 1999. This is a political
time bomb that will not go away—the public will become even more
business literate.

The re-education of existing directors, and the education of future
ones, will depend on very different stances being taken by shareholders and politicians on their assessed competences. Corporate governance has not been a serious module on any major MBA program. The
only alternative of which I am aware—an action-learning-based
Master's in Company Direction at the UK's Leeds Metropolitan
University—has had a good start but stands on its own. The London
Institute of Directors' Chartered Director Initiative looks very promis-
ing, especially as it has already been copied by the Japanese
Management Association. Nevertheless, as the pattern of repeated

CEO failure is increasingly noted by shareholders and the public alike, and action is demanded to improve their performance rather than their executive packages, international remedies will be demanded.

In the end, boards of directors will re-establish their credibility only by recapturing their role of properly overseeing the tasks of direction-giving and prudent control. To do this effectively, the chief executive—or more properly managing director—role needs to be moderated, and the other directors' roles enhanced, in the minds of all players. This starts with acknowledgment of the supremacy of the board of directors.

Answers to the six basic questions for a director
(These are based on UK and Commonwealth law.)

1 Anyone "purporting to be" or "holding themselves out to be" a director will assume the same liabilities as a member of the board of directors. Using the title "director of…" does not let you off the hook. It is, therefore, very unwise to give the title "director" as part of a promotion if the person is not going to become a board member.

2 The only limitation on the liability of a director of a company limited by share capital is on the paid-up shareholder capital. All directors have unlimited liability for their actions.

3 There are no such terms as "executive director" or "nonexecutive director" at law. All directors are equal and each has a single vote.

4 The prime loyalty of a director is to the company as a separate legal personality. The argument is that if the directors are ensuring the long-term health of their company, they are delivering their fiduciary duty.

5 Senior executives and external consultants who directly influence a particular decision without the board members having time and capacity to debate the decision among themselves can be considered to be "shadow directors" and are therefore liable.

6 No one knows. There is no legal precedent or statute at present. The usual advice is to act as though the relevant company laws provide best-practice guidance, but this has not been tested in the courts.

CHAPTER FOUR

The Ten Directoral Duties

Back to Legal Basics

ONE OF THE GREAT ADVANTAGES OF the current corporate governance movement is that the main debates and developments are happening between the *practitioners*. It is a fresh field where major developments are led by the directors and where currently the consultants, politicians, and academics are also-rans. Long may it stay so.

In this chapter I want to show that while we must give *rights* to powerful decision-makers in our enterprises, we must also balance them with more explicit *duties* to the owners and to the wider community. Such duties must be designed to counterbalance any assumption of absolute directoral rights. There are practical and pragmatic ways of so doing, which I will examine here.

As directors we build on the foundation of balancing the eternal dilemma of how to drive our enterprises forward while keeping them under prudent control. However, as our wider community has less reason to trust directoral judgment, probity, and ethics, and as public awareness grows that direction-givers are not necessarily trained to competence, so the demand grows for increasing directoral duties and for legislation. Many directors resent this, but if they want to continue to exercise directoral rights and privileges there is likely to be no escape from accepting the consequent duties.

In this chapter I want to discuss the fundamental ideas, values, and expected behavior of directors that are known to lead to more effective board performance and so to better business performance, and particularly to added shareholder value.

The Legal Foundation of Boards

Let us go back to basics again, specifically to the legal basis for the underlying theory and structure of boards. Historically, the effectiveness of the concept of the joint-stock company with limited liability is acknowledged as the basis of modern capitalism. By the mid-nineteenth century the original, closely held ownership of companies proved insufficient either to direct or control the growing complexity of businesses. "Managers" began to be employed as agents of the owners and to liaise with both customers and workforce. This model still holds good in many companies, although the more active term "executive" is more commonly used now.

However, as businesses expanded further so did the need for capital. With the original owners often unable to supply it, the search spread wider. As the original ownership was diluted, legislation in the form of company law was needed to regulate the relationship between the managers and the more distant equity owners. Spreading the ownership more widely was, and still is, often wrongly seen as getting access to "free" capital that could be exploited at will by the managers.

The legislation was based on reinforcing two simple and powerful ideas. First, that the company had a separate legal personality, for example that it could sue and be sued in its own name and sign contracts. This seemed to many an elegant expedient.

Indeed Adam Smith, in the revolutionary year of 1776, acknowledged the profundity of the joint-stock, limited liability concept. Yet he also had grave reservations about it. Few nowadays realize that he was professor of moral philosophy, and later political economy, at Glasgow University and had written a book on the *Theory of Moral Sentiment* before writing *The Wealth of Nations*. His interest was not merely in what we call "economics," i.e., the creation of wealth, but also in its distribution in society for good. In his mind the two had to be connected if one was to have an equitable society. Smith was writing in good intellectual company: *The Rights of Man* by Tom Paine helped frame the US Declaration of Independence, and Jean-Jacques Rousseau had been influential with his *Social Contract* in the drive toward the French Revolution. Over two centuries later it is astonishing to consider just what an effect these three thinkers had on creating the foundations for, and governance of, our modern world.

Adam Smith was concerned that in the very long run, and centuries before the anti-globalization movement, the new corporations could over time gain the power to destabilize society through:

* Unlimited life.
* Unlimited size.
* Unlimited power.
* Unlimited license.

He therefore argued they could potentially become as much a force for harm as for good. Smith realized that such companies would need effective regulation within, through a controlling group elected by the owners, and without, through the legislators, in addition to the important balancing role of market forces—his oft-quoted "invisible hand."

The second and equally radical idea reinforced by the legislation was the development of a board of directors comprising "merchant adventurers." The concept of a board of directors under a governor developed with the formation of the East India Company in 1600. This (royal) chartered company was based on the novel assumption that previously autonomous merchant adventurers would do better to organize their funds collectively and become owners of a "joint stock" company. It was only after the mid-eighteenth century that the idea of the company itself having a separate legal personality and limited liability was accepted. This paved the way for boards of directors becoming more common.

Perhaps even more radical was the later idea that the mid-Victorian owners should elect a mixed group from their members who at the very moment of their election would swap their primary loyalty away from the shareholders to the company as that separate legal entity. Over the last 100 years this has often been more honored in the breach than in reality. However, as public opinion and social, political, and economic pressures change, as shown in Chapter 2, so this fundamental notion of the power and responsibilities of the board of directors is being taken much more seriously again. The rapidly growing raft of litigation against boards and individual directors in this area will ensure that it will be better respected in future.

The Ethical Foundation of Boards

What are the key directoral duties that, when exercised effectively by the board, will have the owners, stakeholders, and the public at large only too happy to bestow generous rights on all members of the board of directors—their continuing license to operate?

It is worth spending a few moments thinking about duties and their implied ethical basis, including the powerful rights that are granted with them. Had I written that sentence before the Enron scandal most people would have either yawned or laughed out loud in disbelief that there is any relationship between business, governance, and ethics. Post-Enron a major change is occurring in the public mind. The three values of corporate governance—accountability, probity, and transparency—are being viewed in a much more positive light.

To define my terms, I take "ethics" to be the values determining the relationship between one person and another, the deep values that help hold a society together and are made manifest through people's behavior toward each other. "Values" are a belief in action seen through thoughts and, especially, behavior. If a set of values is generally accepted then, by definition, there will be an acceptance of "right" and "wrong," "good" and "bad" in that society.

That seems to be where the problem lies with much of current business thinking. We have bred many clever people paid large sums of money to do things that are unprofessional and unethical, even if not actually illegal. We have encouraged the ability to be rewarded for doing wrong—and are now paying the price for it.

It is strongly argued by some philosophers that the West lives in a "post-ethical" society where everything is relative and there are no firm guiding values other than self-interest. I pray not, or the West is doomed to historical decline. This is especially true if the basic relationship between people ceases to be tolerance, thoughtfulness to others, civility, and obeying fair law—and instead becomes "anything goes, provided I don't get caught." That would signal what the Australians would call the "white anting" of society: a hollowing out of our bonding systems, so that though the exterior does not show signs of major attack, it is only when the edifice collapses that people realize that something is fundamentally wrong.

The Ten Duties of a Professional Director

In 1997 I was one of the founder members of the Commonwealth Association for Corporate Governance (CACG), under the leadership of Geoffrey Bowes of the New Zealand Institute of Directors and Michael Gillibrand of the Commonwealth Secretariat. The 54 heads of government of the Commonwealth (bound closely together by a common legal system, the English language, and trade) had already agreed that to sustain and energize economic and social development in their countries they would greatly benefit from the application of effective and rigorous corporate governance, financial reporting and auditing systems, banking supervision systems, and the better implementation of systems of civil law.

Like most of the "developing" world, many of the Commonwealth countries are in deep economic and social distress. There is a general feeling that previous attempts to resolve these problems through various aid programs and experiments with political and religious ideology had been ineffective. CACG argues that focusing on effective corporate governance through self-help, action learning (homeopathic doses of outside help, rather than lots of well-paid western consultants), self-discipline, the creation of robust national institutions, and an enforced legal framework are most likely to help curb corruption, increase foreign direct investment, reinforce good government, and build self-confidence as the basis of a "civil society." It is accepted that corporate governance alone cannot do this; but in combination with honest accounting figures, effective banking supervision, and the application of just law it can go a long way to creating that civil society. CACG is an important player in these developments as it starts to run its basic director training programs, initially in Africa and the Caribbean.

In 1998 CACG published its *Code of Good Practice for the Board*,[1] which has already caused great interest particularly as it was developed as a multicultural exercise by practitioners across six continents. While this was a necessary first step, it was not sufficient in itself. I was commissioned by CACG and the Commonwealth Secretariat to work on a draft set of globally applicable fundamental duties for directors and boards. What seemed daunting at first turned out to be both challenging and enlightening. I was amazed at how many people were willing to criticize my early drafts constructively—they actually wanted a result. These included many eminent lawyers, including the current UK Attorney General Peter Goldsmith, and many interested directors from five continents. There was a real passion for something to be done, as much in Islamic, Confucian, Taoist, and Hindu-based nations as Christian ones—and this was long before Enron. One QC wrote a plea that as he had recently had to wade through 400 pages of treacly prose on a proposed single clause to an EU law change, he would deem it a miracle if I came in with anything less than a book! We managed ten pages.

The Ten Duties has not been formally published as it has not yet received ratification by the Commonwealth heads of government. Nevertheless, I have permission from CACG to publish it here in draft form to help continue and widen the discussion. The ten directoral duties are designed to be universally applicable. I have tried them also in China, across the Islamic world, in Angola, and in non-Commonwealth South East Asia. I found that the duties were willingly accepted as a useful basis for the development of people's own culturally adapted versions of corporate governance.

The ten duties ask a board, and each director, to behave within the legal and ethical bounds of:

1 The duty of legitimacy.
2 The duty of upholding the three values of corporate governance.
3 The duty of trust.
4 The duty of upholding the primary loyalty of a director.
5 The duty of care.
6 The duty of critical review and independent thought.

7 The duty of delivering the primary roles and tasks of the board.
8 The duty of protecting minority owners' interests.
9 The duty of corporate social responsibility.
10 The duty of learning, developing, and communicating.

My task here is to discuss why each duty has evolved legally, and how they can be turned into best practice for any board in the private or public sectors. From my international experiences I know that understanding and applying the ten directoral duties can make a significant difference to the effectiveness of any board and, therefore, to its ability to add value for both its owners and its stakeholders.

Let us look at each of the ten duties in turn.

1 The Duty of Legitimacy

The duty of legitimacy stresses the importance of staying within national and international law. This may sound so blindingly obvious for any director and board that it should not be worthy of comment. However, with the US and UK governments moving more of company law from the civil to the criminal courts, this duty needs careful study. Nevertheless, many directors find themselves, usually through a lack of proper induction to their role, ignorant of the many aspects of company law for which they are corporately and personally liable. A quick test of this is the brief benchmarking quiz in Chapter 3. I am still surprised by board scores of 90 percent incorrect regardless of nationality, seniority, time as a director, or the nature of the business sector. This is a massive indictment of the lack of directoral training and development.

It has become clear that governments are, very belatedly, willing to use the criminal law against offending directors and executives in a way that has never been seen before. The fact that a director can be sued as personally liable in a growing number of instances—for example in breaking health and safety, environmental pollution, corporate manslaughter, and fraud laws—is only just beginning to be realized by many boards. There is the inevitable cry of "We'll never be able to find enough directors to sit on our boards in future!" The international pendulum is beginning to swing too far in favor of criminalizing directors and will need to be corrected. Yet I feel that the general direction is good, because it was corporately ignorant and incompetent directors who got us into this mess in the first place.

Thus it is highly recommended that a director and board induction program is undertaken, both remedial for current directors and educational for potential directors. It should start with each director being given the appropriate national company law or ordinance, and having the consequences explained to them in detail by the chairman and company secretary before they sign as to their willingness to become a director and so put their personal wealth and liberty on the line.

However, merely comprehending the legislation and regulatory processes is not enough. I am astonished at how few directors have been given—or have read—the specific laws and rules applying to their own organization. There are two basic documents that all directors must understand about their corporation:

❖ The *Memorandum and Articles of Association*, the outcome of the vital legal process that created and maintains their specific company. These define the legal limits of the company's ability to operate, as well as such procedures as voting at annual general and extraordinary general meetings, board selection and dismissal processes, issuing shares, declaring dividends, etc. If these processes are not followed, the board will find itself acting *ultra vires* (beyond the law) and will be held liable by the owners, and especially the regulators, mainly for civil wrongs. It is both the chairman and the company secretary's duty to ensure that due process, derived from the Memorandum and Articles of Association of the company, is followed around the boardroom table at all times.

❖ The *Shareholders' Agreement*. Where it exists this is the contractual document for the owners, not the directors, of the company. Nevertheless, it is crucial that the directors know the broad strategies of the owners—the directoral "license to operate" given to the board. In companies that are closely held—or that have aggressive and greedy shareholders—the Shareholders' Agreement is a crucial document for the directors to understand as it sets out the fundamental aspirations demanded by the owners. It must also be considered carefully in relation to the Memorandum and Articles of Association to ensure continuing legality.

When signing the legal papers to become a director of a company, I insist that a director also signs a note that he or she has received and read the Memorandum and Articles of Association and any relevant Shareholders' Agreement, and makes a declaration of personal interests for the board's Register of Directors' Interests. In addition, stock exchanges in each country and region have their own legal documents for directors that should be issued, read, and acknowledged. For listed companies in the UK this is referred to as the London Stock Exchange's Purple Book.

It is also useful to have a third document read by all directors, the Reserved Powers of the Board. This spells out the decisions that only the board can take and specifies the levels of authority of both directors and managers, so short-circuiting the many squabbles into which boards and executives can get.

Ignorance is no defense at law. I have seen some particularly sad cases of this in subsidiary companies of multinationals who relied on instructions from head office overseas without appreciating that they were operating under different laws in the country in which they were directing.

I have seen even worse cases in charities and not-for-profits. Here good-hearted members of the community agree to be directors and give their time free, or for a tiny stipend, without any proper induction or explanation of their directoral duties and of the implications of liability on their personal wealth. They assume too readily that because they are doing charity work the organization must be well run and honest, and that as they are unpaid they will not be held liable. Neither can be assumed. I have had to give what help I could to distraught directors of religious bodies, school governors, and directors of housing associations when their personal liabilities have been exposed to them, sometimes brutally and with devastating effects on their families. This is not to argue against being a director of a charity or not-for-profit, rather to say that the very least the enterprise can do is ensure that the existing and potential boards, and individual directors, are well briefed.

Corruption

There is a shadow side to legitimacy. A few directors and boards are corrupt; others are led into bribery and corruption (in the more general sense, rather than the psychological abuses of power discussed in the next chapter).

I first became aware of this when working with a group of young, potential directors; HiPos, in the jargon. One was quite distressed as he had been ordered to take a suitcase full of money out of the country to pay bribes to ensure the winning of a contract in the Orient. He was very worried both because this was a criminal act and because, if he were caught, the consequences for him and his family were likely to be severe. We discussed this with his colleagues on the HiPo development program. About three-quarters said that they would do this if ordered to by their boss. The rest said they would not, yet feared the likely effect on their careers. When I raised this with their bosses I was told that this was the normal way of doing business in that part of the world and instructed not to interfere. When I pointed out that it was illegal, and that in such poor countries the misapplication of funds away from their intended use meant that both the country and the contractor lost out, I was met with incredulous stares. Their message was that I was patently mad, bad, and dangerous to know. I did not stay as a consultant with the company.

Corruption comes in many forms, from blatantly bribing a key individual to ensure that you are on a tender list, all the way to paying agent's or consultancy fees to the decision-takers themselves for "work" that is definitely not done. I repeat that the working definition of corruption is "the abuse of office for personal gain." Bribing such an office holder is fundamentally wrong and is illegal in all the countries in which I have worked.

Nevertheless, I am frequently attacked by both western business people and the local office-holders for trying to break their game.

Indeed, the locals often say that this is a key part of their income and that because their local pay is so low they cannot support their families otherwise. This can be horribly true for minor officials, and the use of "dash" in Africa and "tea money" in East Asia is common. It can only be stamped out finally by the eradication of poverty and a fairer distribution of wealth. It is noticeable in a country like South Africa that local executives of major corporations are often paid at the global rate, while the workforce is paid at the local market rate.

It is possible for the providers of external capital to apply concerted international anti-corruption pressure for the acceptance of best practice. About 80 percent of the world's capital is private, so businesses can have a major positive or negative effect on corruption and its consequences. Yet as BP found out, its decision to publish the amounts paid to companies, set against the actual contract costs, caused an uproar when others could do a simple subtraction and deduce the amount of money that "disappeared."

Transparency is a key weapon in countering corruption. A heroic fighting force in this area is Transparency International, based in Berlin and operating globally.[2] Its complex calculations of bribery and corruption, based on hard and soft data from many sources about each major trading nation, provide annual league tables to which more and more investors are turning. See Figure 1 for the 2002 scores on bribery, and Figure 2 for those scores on corruption. Transparency International has set up in many cities around the world and is looking for recruits and monitors to help in its sterling work.

How are others trying to handle what is a growing global issue? The US Foreign Corrupt Practices Act (FCPA) makes it a criminal offense for a US citizen to pay bribes to an official overseas, and the punishment is being extended to non-US citizens working for or with US companies overseas. Many countries are looking to create a similar law. The FCPA is tough and companies wishing to bid for, say, US defense contracts must go through a rigorous vetting process before they are allowed on to the tender lists. This has caused much soul-searching among, for example, European Union companies, which are unused to such "impertinence." They are therefore having to clean up their act, albeit reluctantly. For example, currently a bribe paid

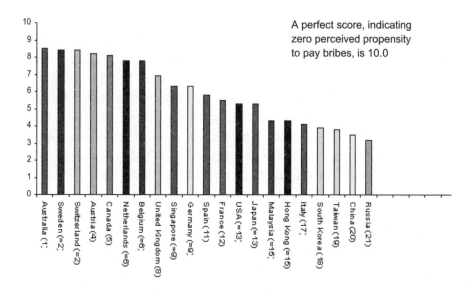

Figure 1 Transparency International's Bribe Payers' Index 2002

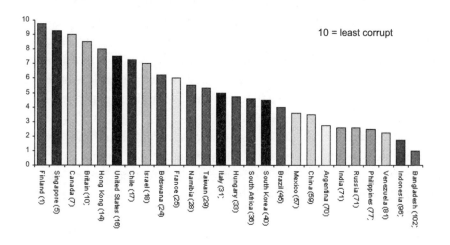

Figure 2 Transparency International's Corruption Index 2002

overseas by a German business person is tax deductible. In most EU countries "fees" paid overseas that have been agreed with the national tax authorities are also tax deductible. This is a hypocritical and pernicious system that must be stopped.

In the stakes for the most draconian anti-bribery laws the UK is making a strong bid. In July 2002 the UK Home Office's Proceeds of Crime Bill proposed that companies convicted of using bribery to win contracts overseas would have both corporate profits and assets seized. This is in addition to fines and penalties imposed from conviction under new anti-corruption laws and is part of the OECD commitment to crack down hard on bribery overseas. The Bill will suggest the creation of an Assets Recovery Agency as part of a wider fight against terrorism, organized crime, and human trafficking. The Bill is too loosely drafted at present and so is facing tough opposition, but the bones of a future legislative approach to bribery and corruption are spelled out clearly.

Some countries have been notoriously bad at coming to terms with institutionalized corruption. China, with its lack of any robust system of commercial law, has a particularly bad reputation, as the Hainan Island scandal demonstrated. At present Kazakhstan is noticeably bad and CalPERS' actions in pulling out of investing in some East Asian and South American countries is symptomatic of a growing concern about the lack of effective corporate governance. Yet investors are fickle creatures and are often driven as much by emotion as logic or ethics. China is still the preferred country for many overseas investors, presumably on the basis that ten million lemmings can't be wrong, despite all the evidence to the contrary.

I have spent nearly 30 years in and around China and love the country dearly, despite its dreadful governance. I remember sitting in an investment conference in Shanghai in the mid-1990s and discussing experiences in China since 1976 with the head of a major US fragrances company. He did not want to hear our message. He had a "China strategy." When asked what it was, he looked me straight in the eye and said, "Bob, there are 1.2 billion people in China. For us that means 2.4 billion armpits. That's all we need to know!" It gives me no pleasure to report that he, along with so many others, did not do well, upset the locals expecting their "tea money," and enraged his shareholders with his writedowns. He has gone the way of all corporate flesh.

The good news is that governments, institutions, and individuals alike are beginning to take action against rampant corruption. The most intriguing proposal, and at the highest level, comes from the billionaire financier and philanthropist George Soros, who has done remarkable work for Central Europe through his Open Society Institute[3] and is now turning his thoughts to the global effects of corruption. He wants international stock exchange regulators to impose new rules that counter corruption by ensuring transparency. Supported by such NGOs as Global Trade Watch,[4] he is demanding that it becomes mandatory for companies investing or contracting overseas to break down their payments, especially royalties and taxes, to individual governments on a country-by-country basis, rather than the situation under current stock exchange rules where companies can consolidate payments to different countries into a single set of accounts.

Soros's interest and anger were aroused when companies were asked to disclose payments to the government of war-riddled Angola. It was estimated that some $1 billion had bypassed the Angolan Treasury controls altogether since 1997. Soros pointed out strongly that this money could have gone to reduce poverty and jump-start economic growth. Instead it was stolen. Oil accounts for an estimated 90 percent of the country's $5 billion annual budget and it was from the oil account that much money was thought to have disappeared. Among the first countries to sign up to Soros's initiative are Angola itself and Kazakhstan.

Energy company BP has so far been the only company to agree that it would disclose its tax payments to the Angolan government, a decision that generated much anger and the threat of termination of its oil contracts. There are undoubted risks in taking unilateral action in a competitive world. A better approach would be to ensure that the world's stock exchanges, the US Securities and Exchange Commission, the UK's Financial Services Authority, the European Parliament, and other bodies demand legislation requiring the breakdown of such payments in companies' quarterly and annual accounts. Soros thinks that this would capture all the major large resource companies, especially oil, gas, and mining, which would be very unlikely to delist from the exchanges. The campaign is to be applauded and encouraged, but it will be a long, and tough, haul.

2 The Duty of Upholding the Three Values of Corporate Governance

For centuries the three fundamental values of all forms of good governance have been:

❖ Accountability.
❖ Openness.
❖ Probity.

In corporate governance terms the three values can be stated with more precision:

❖ Accountability to the owners.
❖ Honest dealing within and without the board.
❖ Transparency of risk-assessment and decision-taking processes to the owners.

We look here at the implications of the three values in more detail.

Accountability to the owners

The owners' appointment of a board of directors is based on the assumption that the directors will be fully accountable, corporately (as the board has an independent legal status from the company) and individually, for their actions on behalf of those owners. In the days when external environmental changes were relatively slow, a system of reporting at an annual general meeting, where profits and dividends were announced and few questions asked, was adequate. As communities tended to be small and closely geographically defined, it was relatively easy for the shareholders to have an overview of both the competence of the directors and the operational performance of the managers. In addition, the growing use of a group of external, independent monitors—the financial auditors—helped ensure fair dealing by the board.

Curiously, in the UK and Commonwealth countries, neither the board nor the auditors needs to state in the annual report that the business is a going concern and can, therefore, be said to have good prospects of continuing to survive and grow. The notable exception is South Africa, where this statement is a legal requirement. The UK and some other countries are seeking to include this in a revision of company law; similarly, the New York Stock Exchange is proposing that CEOs and financial officers not only sign quarterly accounts but are personally liable for ensuring statements of any other matters of which the owners should be aware, including the continuity of the company.

With the growing environmental turbulence—political, physical environmental, economic, social, technology and design development, and world trade—the comforting beliefs in the sufficiency of an annual report and a board that gave a guaranteed dividend and gentle equity growth have gone. The need for the board, rather than the managing director, to be the key source of regular business performance information for owners, regulators, and stakeholders has grown much more important. Half-yearly reports to the owners are fine. Quarterly reports are pointless for the general investor. Reporting systems cannot be that accurate or positive in such a short timespan, unless you hope to live in a fairyland where ratios and profits always rise for the better. Dr. Pangloss may have believed that "everything is for the best in the best of all possible worlds," but the sane investor does not.

Nowadays monthly internal reporting and auditing systems require both much more accuracy and linkage into an information system that allows the board to see the *pattern* of movement of all the figures, rather than merely the figures themselves in isolation. Directors must ensure that the prudent control side of their role is in place. As the limited liability of the company refers to the paid-up shareholders only, there is no doubt at law that the board and the directors have unlimited liability and so must spend significant time in getting their accountabilities right. Not that many directors have realized this—yet.

The role of the company secretary

Ensuring that the proper procedures of the board are carried out in a timely manner is the duty of both the chairman and the company secretary. This latter job is not seen by many boards as a professional appointment. Often some poor director is given it as an additional, if unimportant, task. Nevertheless, being a company secretary is a highly professional role.

Legally the company secretary is not a member of the board, but an officer of it. He or she must supervise due process under company law to ensure that, for example, the correct annual returns are made to the relevant authorities at the right times; the board follows proper pro-cedure under its Memorandum and Articles of Association; board agendas are drawn up for board meetings, full minutes are kept, and minutes and board papers are circulated in a timely manner so that directors have time to read and absorb them, and to ensure both their accuracy and that appropriate actions are being taken by the executives.

A major bulwark to stopping the erosion of good board practice and, ultimately, corruption is to ensure that the chairman and com-pany secretary trust each other. Without such trust, the board will under-perform and affect shareholder value. There is also a useful reminder in the *Cadbury Report on the Financial Aspects of Corporate Governance* that in UK and Commonwealth law every director has an absolute right to put any matter they wish to discuss on the board's agenda via the company secretary. While it is good manners to inform the chairman, it is not strictly necessary.

Honest dealing within and without the board

Honesty within the board

Honest dealing or probity is the second key value of effective corporate governance. It is the bastion of board competence and against board corruption, including the abuse of power and privilege around the boardroom table. It is based on mutual trust, having confidence in your colleagues. This can be developed, but must never be assumed until tested thoroughly. The key question is how to ensure that the board is eternally vigilant and so able to keep directors under reasonable control.

The CACG *Code of Good Practice for the Board* shows two useful approaches that I feel are worth repeating here. First, it states in Section 5:

Directors at all times have a duty and responsibility to act honestly.

A director should not obtain, attempt to obtain, or accept any bribe, secret commission or illegal inducement of any sort; and this should be actively discouraged throughout the organisation, with appropriate sanctions where it is found to have taken place.

And in Section 7 the guidelines state:

The Board should endeavour to ensure that the organisation is financially viable and properly managed.

The personal interest of a director, or persons closely associated with a director, must not take precedence over those of the organisation and its shareholders.

There are some simple actions that can be taken by any board to avoid the worst problems of dishonest dealing. First, have some basic rules built into the Memorandum and Articles of Association. The roles and tasks of the board, of the chairman, and of individual directors and the company secretary can be specified (curiously, they are normally not).

Separately, a board's Standing Orders can insist on the following:

❖ A Register of Directors' Interests that is kept up to date by the company secretary, with the onus on directors to make accurate declarations or face board suspension.
❖ An agreed board behavior that all directors will declare their own, and close family and friends', interests in any item under discussion.
❖ Directors must withdraw from the discussion of any item under discussion after their declaration of interest in it, unless there is unanimous and recorded board agreement to do otherwise.
❖ Directors will not vote on any item that affects their personal interests.
❖ The Register of Directors' Interests should be open to inspection by shareholders at any time.

These can come as quite a shock to people put on to the board as a "representative" director. At law there is no such thing. Directors' first duty from the moment of their appointment is to the company, not to the people who elected them. This puts many shareholder, worker, bank, pension fund, political party, and other "director-representatives" in a legally clear, but politically very delicate, position.

Honesty without the board

Much of this has been dealt with under Duty 1. However, it is worth stressing here that when dealing with overseas players it is advisable to use the highest-practice rules, rather than to go for local customs. In a competitive world this is always difficult, so the question comes back to the fundamental ethical values of shareholders and directors. Many of these will be backed up by deeply held family and religious beliefs. As "ethical investment" funds grow apace it is becoming a little easier to take a principled stand on where a company's overseas investments go, as, for example, Indonesian logging companies have found when they tried to raise capital on the UK stock exchange. However, corruption is always with us. At its worst it stops inward investment into the country, as for instance Nigeria, Cambodia, and North Korea have found to their cost.

Much corruption comes out of sheer directoral ignorance of the law rather than conscious chicanery. Again, a simple start is to set up a Register of Directors' Interests (and those of their immediate family and friends), and to check this at the start of each board meeting. This too should be open to inspection by the owners at any time. At each board meeting the chairman could then check each item for discussion against the declaration of interests of each board member, senior executives, and any alternate directors or shadow directors present. The board minutes must accurately reflect the declarations, discussions, and votes.

Transparency of the decision-taking process to the owners

Many directors, especially new ones, are horrified by the lack of rigor in their board's decision-making processes. They flinch at the dearth of agreed board procedures for information collection and testing, idea generation, risk assessment, critical review, strategic thinking, decision-taking, and values testing. I shall deal with the processes in depth in Chapter 7.

What many new directors find even worse is that these processes are obscured from the shareholders. This is not to say that shareholders should participate in all decisions; if that were the case there would be no need for directors. What is being argued here is that the shareholders should be aware that there is an agreed, and transparent, process by which decisions are taken by the board, and that the consequences of those decisions will, through the board and director appraisal process, allow the shareholders to decide finally who will be voted back as directors at the annual general meeting.

Many current directors argue that you cannot run a business in this way and that it is their collective experience that allows suitable decisions to be made. The counter argument is that in a turbulent world where strategic decisions are increasingly more likely to "bet the business," a group of experienced people with similar ages, social, academic, professional, and political backgrounds is unlikely to have sufficient *diversity* in its thinking to take wise decisions. Bill Morris, Secretary-General of the UK Transport and General Workers' Union, refers to such boards as "male, pale and stale." If these directors are also in thrall to the chairman or managing director, the experience base for wise decision-taking is usually too small. Opaqueness of board decision-taking processes is a natural consequence of this lack of broad perspective.

More diversity on boards needs to be coupled with more effective accountability and honest dealing to ensure higher-quality decisions. In the UK matters came to a head for boards of London Stock Exchange listed companies with the publication of the Turnbull Report.[5] This insists that every board explains to the owners its risk-assessment and consequent decision-making processes. If it does not, then it is obliged to state in its annual report why it is not doing so—"comply or explain." Needless to say, this has caused consternation on many boards; and some very bland initial annual statements. However, the owners are now expecting to hear from their boards on this critical task and will not be tolerant for long. Turnbull reflects the developing spirit of seeking board performance, and much greater clarity in the ways in which the directors add shareholder value.

This is borne out by the publication of two other reports. The earlier Rutteman Report[6] on systems of internal financial control seems to have caused as much fluttering in the public dovecotes as Turnbull did in the private sector, although not as much action.

In 2001 the Myners' Report[7] was published, a review into institutional investment commissioned by the UK Treasury. Myners' survey showed alarmingly that 62 percent of pension fund trustees and 33 percent of pension scheme administrators had no professional qualifications in finance or investment. Fewer than half of the trustees were graduates and in their first year in post just over 25 percent had one day's training or less for the job; 43 percent had only one or two days' training and usually spent fewer than three hours preparing for investment matters on behalf of the fund.

Myners recommends that pension trustees should be paid, become more professional (there is a ten-point voluntary code attached to the report), and be measured for performance. In terms of transparency, he suggests that their annual reports should have a rigorous statement of investment principles and explain more carefully to their owners their decision-making processes.

These three recent UK reports are highly significant as they are a good illustration of the gathering pace of the move into the second stage of corporate governance development—board performance issues—following the board compliance issues of the Cadbury, Greenbury, and Hampel Reports. They are each radical in their own way and point strongly to the necessary professionalization of the role of both directors and trustees.

The big question is always: "Where do we start?" The good news is that the three values of corporate governance are easily translated into observable behavior and are, therefore, assessable and can form the basis of a board's annual appraisal system. That this happens so rarely at present is a sad indication of the present lack of professionalism of most boards and trustees.

3 The Duty of Trust

Directors are charged by law to hold their company "in trust" for the future. This long-term fiduciary duty is a key aspect of the directoral role. Yet in turbulent times it sits uneasily with the wish of some shareholders to take their money quickly and run. If they are significant shareholders, there will be tension between the directors and the shareholders. While the owners have the absolute right to vote out the directors at an annual or extraordinary general meeting, it is less clear what line the courts might take if the directors could show that the shareholders' demands were likely to threaten the future of the business.

One example is an East Asian group of companies, fully listed on its local stock exchange, but to all intents and purposes owned by a multinational listed in New York and London. During the 1997 "Asian meltdown" the major, but not majority, shareholder demanded cash from its subsidiary to stop the holding company crashing. The local directors saw it as a career-threatening decision to say "no" and so sent the money.

However, local shareholders have threatened action, as this movement of cash is seen as having a destabilizing effect on the company's ability to trade solvently locally and thus is threatening their investment. It is argued that if the shareholders can show that the removal of cash made the company so close to insolvency that it could be accused of "trading recklessly," the directors must have breached their fiduciary duty. This is untested at present and will provide interesting case law if it finally goes to court. It will help define the point at which directors of a company can roll over and say "yes" to what the Chinese call "a big potato," or whether they must always stand up and fight.

4 The Duty of Upholding the Primary Loyalty of a Director

Following from the three values of corporate governance and the duty of trust comes the issue of a director's primary loyalty. As previously mentioned, it is very clear at law. From the moment of someone's election as a director, their primary loyalty must be to the company as a legal entity, rather than to those who appointed them. This can be confusing in the early days for any director, and frustrating for the shareholders, bankers, trade unions, political parties, or community groups who appointed them. The latter's expectations are that "their" representatives will always do their bidding. This cannot be so—unless it can be shown to coincide with the best long-term interests of the company. The immediate needs of the owners must be forgone by directors if these will challenge the future health of the company.

Directing is all about exercising judgment, corporately and individually, and this issue is always a contentious one. It takes a competent chairman to guide a board successfully through the dilemma.

5 The Duty of Care

Directors must exercise their accountabilities, roles, and tasks competently. They must be careful in what they do and how they do it, and ensure that what they decide is for the benefit of the company, not themselves. Hence the new interest in the board's information-selection, idea-generation, risk-assessment, strategic thinking, critical review, decision-taking, and values-testing board processes made manifest in the UK by the acceptance of the Turnbull Report. These processes are dealt with in much greater detail in Chapter 7.

It is essential that all directors know what they are meant to be doing, do it, and are measured on it. The exercise of due care in directing means that five frequently avoided personal demands are now accepted by directors:

❖ The job is not simply a matter of attending board meetings on the day and then saying "yes" or "no" to proposals from the executives.
❖ Directors must give due preparation time to board papers before the meeting.
❖ Sufficient time must be budgeted by directors to fulfill their duty of care.

❖ Directors must be properly inducted, trained to competence, and appraised on a regular basis.
❖ It is therefore impossible for any one director to hold more than four directorships without seriously jeopardizing their duty of care.

At this point there will be squeals of pain and outrage from many existing directors who see being a director as a passive and comfortable lifestyle. Tough. It used to be, but it is no longer. The reciprocal advantage is that directors will need to be paid better (and not by stock options) so that they can devote sufficient time to do a care-full job.

6 The Duty of Critical Review and Independent Thought

This directoral duty can seem highly intimidating to a new—or non-competent—director. The laws behind the duty are that in the UK and Commonwealth the board of directors is treated as a group of equal colleagues under a neutral chairman elected from the directors themselves. Each director, therefore, is expected to be sufficiently self-aware and mature to be able to make their own judgment on the best direction and prudent control systems for the health of the company.

A proper director-induction process under the supervision of the chairman will make this very clear. Indeed, some companies have a formal public ceremony at which an executive will be congratulated on his or her promotion to director. This "rite of passage" ceremony allows the rest of the company to understand that while the director may have some residual executive functions, there will be times when priority must be given to more important directoral matters.

Such rites of passage help with the real fear of many executive directors that in being constructively critical of or opposing their managing director or chairman's ideas, they are committing career suicide. This is understandable, as many executive directors will agree a line to take with the board beforehand and then stick together resolutely to defend it. They are not then acting as collegial directors, but as a faction. An effective chairman understands this and has rules of engagement that allow neutral time to debate ideas and especially the sources of strategic information without prisoners being taken or grudges stored for future use. Only then will the board go into the strategic decision-taking process.

The chairman should be particularly aware of any pre- or post-board meeting "beatings-up" by the managing director on the other side of the boardroom door, and have systems for checking this regularly. The open relationship between the chairman as "boss of the board" and the managing director as "boss of daily operations" must be cultivated and sustained in any successful company. What many directors fail to understand is that they have equal votes around the boardroom table—and are obliged to use them. Add to this the right to raise any item for the agenda and it can be seen that they are in a more powerful position than many realize. Their ignorance, and their unwillingness to take hard decisions or defend agreed values-based positions, allow them the seemingly easy option of saying that they simply could not oppose their managing director, even when they knew a proposition was flawed or the information wrong. In the US they might now get 20 years in jail for this. When things go wrong both shareholders and the courts ask increasingly: "Then why are you purporting to act as directors and not simply executives? Don't you understand the difference?"

The duty of independent critical thought does not seek to undermine the managing director. It helps put this role into its proper perspective. When the directors leave the boardroom those with executive functions will revert to executing the board's decisions. The managing director is still the boss of the business's operations, but they should not make policy or strategy decisions on their own, to later sell them to the board on a "take-it-or-leave-it" basis. A wise managing director will have agreed with their executives precisely what will be put to the board and explained to them the areas of doubt and risk that the executives see as for discussion. A wise board will question these very carefully. A wise director, executive or non-executive, will ensure that no information is held back in this process. The consequences of holding back such information in the medium and long term are frequently disastrous.

7 The Duty of Delivering the Primary Roles and Tasks of the Board

The roles of the board can be described as four interlinked dilemmas. As is the nature of dilemmas, each proposition is in opposition to the other. That is why the board's decision-taking role is never easy. Directing is intellectually tough work. It is the board's job to exercise its best judgment on how to balance, and rebalance, each proposition depending on the dynamics of the business's changing external and internal environment. There are few easy options in directoral decision-making.

The four directoral dilemmas[8] of the board are:

❖ Driving the enterprise forward, while keeping it under prudent control.
❖ Being required to be sufficiently aware of the workings of the business to be responsible for its actions, while having time to develop a longer-term, more objective view of developments outside the business.
❖ Being sensitive to short-term, local demands, while balancing these against broader regional, national, and international trends.
❖ Being focused on the commercial needs of the business, while acting responsibly to other stakeholders in your society.

To turn these board roles into board tasks it is necessary to subdivide them again into four active processes, as shown in the learning board model[9]:

❖ Formulating policy.
❖ Thinking strategically.
❖ Supervising management.
❖ Ensuring accountability.

There is more detail on these in Chapter 7.

8 The Duty of Protecting Minority Owners' Interests

This can be seen as an extension of the honest dealing aspects of the second duty. In most developed economies this is not a major issue, as the regulators are making it more and more difficult for minority shareholders to be treated with contempt. Some Memoranda and Articles of Association reflect this already, as do Shareholder Agreements, and growing legal protection is being offered. Reports like Myners' and Turnbull show that this will also be taken more seriously when the board's decision-making processes are more openly dissected.

Some activist fund managers—e.g., CalPERS, LENS, Hermes—and critics such as PIRC are now making explicit their wish not to trade on the margin, but to seek out value in underperforming boards and companies and then to work with them in investing for the medium-term benefit of all. If this is delivered, the rights of minorities are likely to be better spotlighted as part of improved board decision-making processes. If you add the millions of activist pensioners and their access to the internet, then the old propensity for directors to act as if they really did own the company and were doing shareholders a favor in even publishing an annual report must die rapidly.

However, in countries where the rule of commercial law is weak minority shareholders have a tough time, although even here there are glimmers of light. This is especially true where privatization is underway, or where the government is seeking substantial funds from foreign investors as part of its long-term economic development policy. While small shareholders still tend to be treated like dirt, there are signs that governments are beginning to take the concept of effective corporate governance seriously, are using or implementing the appropriate personal property laws, and in a few cases are now reconciled to allowing ombudsmen, or international arbitration in disputes. The new Codes of Conduct for Corporate Governance from, for example, CACG, World Bank, and reports from the UN, OECD, and European Union should help greatly here, but it will be a very long haul, unless Nell Minow's concept of "shareholder suffrage" becomes law.

9 The Duty of Corporate Social Responsibility

Corporate social responsibility is a fast-growing and highly controversial area where it is easy to take an extreme position and much more difficult to hold a balanced and pragmatic line. Yet this is what any board must do if its enterprise is to survive. At one extreme we have the argument for the supremacy of the free market and the absolute right to do whatever a board wishes within the law (although even Adam Smith had doubts here). Such free marketeers argue that if there are no existing laws, or the law is not enforced, a board should exploit the situation to the full by maximizing profitability and seeking a monopoly position "for the benefit of their shareholders."

At the other extreme are anti-capitalist groups who see international trade as essentially evil; international companies as a conscious plot to repress labor, human rights, and the development of local economies; and the developed world as another conscious plot to thwart the natural human tendencies of cooperation, love, and stable-state, even rustic, economies. The reliance on part-read and digested tracts from the failed Marxist system, plus an overly romantic view of William Morrisian, utopian socialism ("When Adam delved and Eve span, who was then the gentleman?") are as much an extreme as the free marketeers' position.

In the middle ground are many corporations and individuals who see the need to balance the creation of wealth with direct, and indirect, improvement of the social conditions of everyone. This is much closer to Adam Smith's position on the thoughtful creation and distribution of wealth. A growing element of such thought is the idea that the alleviation of poverty is essential for a richer and more stable world. Poverty is both economic and emotional, and is to be found as much in the "developed" as the "developing" world. This approach to wealth creation opposes any form of authoritarianism and does not reject capitalism—indeed it sees it as the only proven system for generating wealth—but seeks to ensure that the wealth so created can have socially beneficial outcomes for the many.

Thus a response from thoughtful companies (and there are many such) has been to develop the concept of "corporate social responsibility," a conscious move away from the hard-line Berle and Means position on capitalism toward one accepting that a growing mixture of pensioner activists and worker/shareholders, plus significantly more social legislation, means that a company cannot rely on being measured only on its financial performance. They accept that a company cannot run riot with unlimited license.

In a lecture in 1992 at the Royal Society of Arts in London, Charles Handy asked: "What is a company for?"[10] After healthy debate this led to the formation of the Centre for Tomorrow's Company,[11] which has produced some excellent projects and reports, particularly on the rise of the power stakeholders, the notion of the "inclusive company," and the idea that companies in future will need a regularly reviewed license to operate that takes account of their social contribution as well as their financial outputs.

These ideas are creating great interest internationally. For example, I find that in the UK the vast majority of directors with whom I speak are now much more aware of their corporate responsibility to obey the anti-pollution laws, ensure the effectiveness of their health and safety at work procedures, acknowledge the growing raft of rights legislation, and avoid corporate manslaughter charges. You can argue that this has only been brought about by legislation and the consequent fining of sufficient companies and jailing of directors to concentrate their minds wonderfully. I am more optimistic than that. I find that most directors have wanted to be more ethical in their approach to business, but had neither the language (which tended to be mainly religious and offputting) nor the moral courage to do so alone. Legislation is merely making their transition easier. UK directors may grumble about their freedom to manage (notice, not to *direct*) being affected, but most accept that their world will in future be bounded by more than just financial considerations and that in the long run this will be mutually beneficial for all.

Corporate social responsibility will increasingly be built into directors' business calculations. This is practical, as it is an intrinsic aspect of effective board risk assessment, and it is measurable. The French supermarket group Carrefour in its *Sustainability Report 2001* shows how it is encouraging everything from fair trade to eliminating genetically modified organisms from its animal feed products. In measurement terms it is trying, for example, to raise its volume of organic coffee sales from the present 54 tonnes, which it bought in Mexico for 30 percent more than the market price to encourage local producers, and it has tightly specified terms for reducing atmospheric emissions from its own cold storage units. Similarly, the Danish pharmaceutical company Novo Nordisk has listed in its annual report such measures as impact on the environment, people and societies; animal welfare; energy and water usage efficiency; regulatory compliance (which lists all breaches of environmental pollution and gives a medium-term target of zero).

Three further examples show what can be done. After a bad start with the *Brent Spar* oil rig dismantling problem and the Ogoniland/Ken Saro Wiwa Niger Delta tragedy, the board of oil, gas, and chemicals multinational Royal Dutch/Shell Group has learned that its "science and reason only" approach to corporate issues does not work in a wider, more emotional world. It created very bad publicity, with consequent significant reputation risk, political damage, and possible longer-term economic ill-effects.

Shell now recognizes much more consciously that, as a major international investor and employer, it has a positive role to play in both economic and social development through its choice of investments and corporate behavior, especially in environmental improvement and in preventing bribery, corruption, and the misapplication of funds. It can do this while simultaneously protecting and developing its owners' (often now pension funds) interests.

First under Mark Moody-Stewart and then taken forward by the present chairman of the committee of managing directors, Phil Watts, Shell has set out to reposition itself and its reputation by accepting its corporate social responsibility. It has developed the concept of the *triple bottom line*[12] so that it can now report to its owners, and the wider world, its independently audited progress on:

❖ Financial performance.
❖ Physical environmental performance.
❖ Corporate social responsibility performance.

The first report was published in 2001 as *People, Planet and Profits*. This is much more than merely a PR exercise as it affects all aspects of the business, especially its planning and budgeting rounds. Targets and standards are set for all three bottom lines for the period in question. All three outputs then have independent, external auditors appointed who report back as part of the annual auditing process.

This is a heroic attempt to move the whole argument about corporate social responsibility forward and so become more transparent to the shareholders and the broader world in which Shell exists. The company recognizes that in future corporations will have to work within a framework of growing social legislation in many countries, and that it will be used increasingly by legislators as an instrument of national and international policy for economic and social advancement. Many directors in other companies still see Shell's stance as ridiculous, unnecessary, and a wild over-reaction to groups of "lefty wimps." I feel that Shell is learning to get it right for the future in corporate social responsibility terms, and is rebuilding the social capital, and its license to operate, that it dented so badly in the mid-1990s.

The second example is Rio Tinto plc (formerly the RTZ Corporation), an international mining and minerals extraction company. It has had mixed PR for many years, despite frequently being rated in surveys in the upper quartile of corporate social responsibility. It now has a policy that when it operates in any country with laxer laws than the world's best practice, it will work to the highest levels of practice rather than sink to the lowest.

Many rivals have made derisory comments about additional costs and assumed lower shareholder returns. Rio Tinto responds that its actions show a marginal impact in the short term, but that its policy is much more important for the generation of medium- and long-term shareholder value. It has been made a "preferred partner" with a growing number of countries and investment consortia. This is a good example of a board taking a strategic view of its fiduciary duty and balancing its long-term payoffs with shareholders' immediate demands.

The third example is energy group BP plc, which is rolling out the *BP Ethical Conduct Policy*.[13] This publication and implementation program follows on from political risk and business problems in such countries as Russia, Algeria, Angola, and Kazakhstan. It is being taken seriously within the organization as a global scheme and hopes to use BP's African companies as pilot projects, attempting to develop all the African boards to link much improved corporate governance with the Ethical Conduct Policy, backed by proposed serious sanctions on any executives breaking the code.

And in case detractors think that they can sit back, sneer, and let the corporate social responsibility brigade fail under the weight of their assumed greater costs, let me fire across their bows the recent chilling indictment of Unocal Corporation in California. The original suit was brought in 1996 on behalf of 15 Burmese whose village was close to a pipeline being built to move natural gas from the Yadana offshore field to Thailand. The $1.2 billion project, which was completed in 1998, was a joint venture between Unocal of the US, Total of France, the Petroleum Authority of Thailand, and the Myanmar (formerly Burmese) government.

In 2002 the US company and directors stood accused in Los Angeles County of alleged human rights abuses committed by the government of Myanmar during the joint-venture development of a gas field. A judge has ruled that Unocal should face vicarious liability, which holds that business *partners* are responsible for each other's behavior in a joint venture. This will be the first time that a US company has been tried in a US court for alleged abuses of workers abroad. These workers were said to have been forced to perform hard labor against their will and suffered abuses for the benefit of the business venture. If Unocal is found guilty, the International Labor Rights Fund, which is pursuing the case, will ask the jury for $1 billion in damages.

Stephen Davis, editor of *Corporate Watch*, which reports weekly on international corporate governance issues, says:

> *Companies are going to have to take more account of the social consequences of their operations. Critics are learning to use a wide variety of tools to bring them to account especially for slave labour and human rights abuses. Multinationals are at risk whenever they operate outside their home market. They risk entanglement with*

governments that are abusing their citizens or getting involved in situations where human rights aren't protected. Companies will have to take protection from the board level down.

The introduction of the *Financial Times'* FTSE4Good index[14] is a significant sign of the times.

To reinforce this warning, in many countries there is a growing "stakeholder rights" movement, including employees, customers, suppliers, protectors of the physical environment and of the local communities, who combine in many ways to give the corporation a currently unofficial license to operate. While this is seen as a highly dangerous precedent by some directors and executives, such thinking is beginning to be reflected in proposed legislation in Europe and Asia. Such movements are advocating possibly annual appraisal of the whole corporation to be carried out through the auditing process, in a very similar manner to the triple bottom line approach. Only by passing on all three bottom lines could the business be given its license and so continue as a going concern.

Whether there is yet the national political will for such all-encompassing laws to be passed is a matter for speculation. However, most of the necessary laws are already in place in Europe to enforce the idea. Directors are paid in part to watch the evolving future environment for "weak signals" that they then monitor and discuss to develop appropriate strategies. It strikes me that the very notion of a license to operate is a clear and strong indicator of how the future of corporate social responsibility is likely to develop over the next decade.

In addition, at the World Summit on Sustainability in Johannesburg in August 2002 a group of ten of Europe's top institutional investors agreed to be bound by a checklist of conditions on sustainable development—the London Principles—which were developed by the City of London and the UK's Department for the Environment, Food and Rural Affairs. The seven principles are:

❖ To provide access to finance and risk management.
❖ To promote transparency and high standards of corporate governance.

❖ To reflect the cost of environmental and social risks in financial products.
❖ To use equity ownership to promote efficient and sustainable asset use.
❖ To provide access to finance for developing environmental technologies.
❖ To use equity ownership to promote corporate social responsibility.
❖ To provide financial products to disadvantaged and developing communities.

These will be promoted globally under a Memorandum of Understanding with the UN Environmental Programme Financial Initiative. Other countries are being invited to join.

My final point on the duty of corporate social responsibility is that it puts the preferred EU or "Rhenish" model of corporate governance in a poor light. While that model claims social responsibility as its guiding objective, the reality of its inflexible labor laws, unwieldy and slow consultation processes, a bias against wealth creators and so increased unemployment, lack of fiscal and budgetary control, and fiscally impossible generous early retirement and other social benefits suggests a Faustian deal by EU politicians over four decades to maintain the status quo. This now threatens the economic and social stability of the EU itself. In my view it would be far better for EU companies to work within a looser social framework that would allow them to generate more wealth, thus leading to less unemployment, while being monitored on the total effects of their corporate social responsibility through the triple bottom line approach.

10 The Duty of Learning, Developing, and Communicating

If the idea of corporate social responsibility is seen by many to be controversial, the idea that a board of directors has a duty to learn continuously from its decisions and actions, to develop and appraise its members regularly and rigorously, and to maintain effective two-way communication with the rest of their business, its customers, its suppliers, and its stakeholders, must sound even more radical.

It is still assumed by too many directors that the reward of a directorship is simply the acknowledgment of the end of a long and successful executive or professional career, not the beginning of a new one. Therefore, they reason, there is no need for them to learn anything new; indeed, their experience will carry them through to a cosy retirement. This long-established corporate myth is under fire for two reasons. First, directoral competence has proved lacking in so many cases that the litigious are out in force to ensure that in future directors will learn and be assessed on it. Second, there is no law that directing is age related. You do not have to be old to be an effective director—you just have to be brave enough to ask intelligently naïve questions and make sound judgments with the answers. It is only when the liability writs start to fly that existing directors may realize that something is wrong, by which time it will be too late for them to learn their roles and tasks because they will already have been held responsible for what has occurred in their name, whether they knew this or not.

Accepting a directorship is no longer an easy option. The legal liabilities alone should give much cause for personal, and family, concern. Taking out director liability insurance is highly recommended, but does not absolve a director from all liability, and the rates are rising alarmingly.

Accepting a directorship *is* the start of a new and challenging career. It does now mean systematic retraining to break away from the old executive and professional behavior so that a more policy-making and strategic thinking approach can be developed.

Chairmen need to be more aware of their duty to ensure that they have proper director and board induction, inclusion, and competence-building processes in place that are tested at least annually by a board and director appraisal process. Such testing of competence has been developed by the Institute of Directors in London to become the world's first formal international examination process for directors, the Chartered Director initiative. Launched in 1999, this written and oral examination process—an assessment of both knowledge and appropriate experience—plus signing a code of conduct and a guarantee of a continuing professional development program, has proved remarkably popular despite its rigor. (There is more on this in Chapter 8.)

Many existing directors claim that their experience is much better than any examination system. They do not want to be reassessed at their age. Is there any good reason for them to be appraised?

Yes. Just as being a good manager or professional does not make you a good director, so having experience of one board (often without any training) does not guarantee directoral competence. The quick quiz on page 70 is a simple but acid test of this.

So unless one is willing to be a little humble and accept that even a very successful executive needs retraining to be an effective, thoughtful director, the chances of making a success of this part of your life are not high. Indeed, many directors report it as a period of frustration when the going gets intellectually and emotionally tough. Rather than learn their new competences, they seek any opportunity to get back to their position of comfort—the apparent certainties of active executive life. Then they try to micro-manage their old executive functions from the board. This feels great to them, but such behavior creates two major organizational problems: failure to learn how to deliver their directoral duties; and blocking the development of those chosen to succeed them at the executive level. Failure to retrain as a director and to budget time to do this effectively is thus both a dereliction of directoral duty and a blockage in the executive's learning system.

Hence the need not only to train as a director but to undertake regular appraisal and continuing professional development, both as a director and as a total board. This raises the question of whether to include the nonexecutive directors. I repeat that there is no such beast at law. All directors are meant to be treated, and trained, equally. There is no guarantee that their experience as either a member of the great and the good or as an executive director on another board will add to the useful diversity of experience on their current board unless this is appraised regularly.

Deep within this duty of learning, developing, and communicating lies the notion that the board of directors should not sit isolated at the top of the organizational pyramid like the gods on Mount Olympus, but rather that they need to sit at the center of two intersecting cycles of business learning. They are at the center of a figure of eight that balances the demands of the outside world (customers, politicians, pressure groups, etc.) with those of the inside (operational) world (staff, suppliers, bankers, etc.), communicating and learning both ways continuously. This takes time, commitment, and skill. The base is the "business brain" and it is to this world that I turn in Chapter 7.

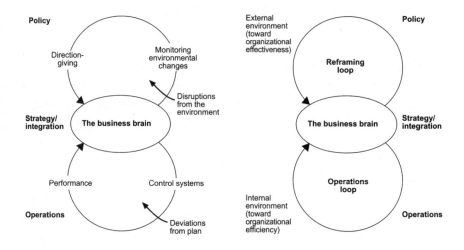

Figure 3 The double loop of learning

I believe that it should be mandatory for every director to sign as to their acceptance of the ten directoral duties at the start of their induction and competence-building process, and that this signing should be reported in the annual report to the owners, together with a record of the number of days each director has spent on continuing professional development. This will then form the basis of the directoral appraisal system and will give comfort to the owners and help build trust both in the board and the board processes.

Part II

Toward Board Performance

CHAPTER FIVE

Why Boards Fail

Power and Corruption on the Board

People of the same trade seldom meet together, even for merriment and diversion, but the conversation ends on a conspiracy against the public, or in some contrivance to raise prices.

Adam Smith, *The Wealth of Nations*

A T THIS POINT THE AUTHORIAL TONE of the book changes from the wide-ranging, analytical, and discursive to a more directoral action focus. I reflect on specific experiences of moving directors from five continents toward the "learning board" approach and the consequent delivery of board performance.

A common public perception of boards is that they are by definition always up to some form of corruption and bribery or another, and if only one could get behind the boardroom door all would be proved. This is not my experience. However, many directors allow ignorance of their roles and tasks and forms of personal and group cowardice to create conditions in which bad things happen. All direction-giving has a moral dimension—good or bad. Currently we are beginning to see exactly which negative directoral values have been allowed to fester over the last three decades. As Warren Buffett put it so succinctly: "It is only in the rinse cycle that you see just how dirty the washing was. We are in the rinse cycle now."

It has never been that difficult for an awake board to grill its executives on both their calculations and the reality of their revenue streams and costs. In the early 1990s Professor Howard Schilit of the American University, Washington DC, was warning of the basic tricks of "creative accounting":

❖ Recording revenues too soon or revenues of questionable quality.
❖ Recording bogus revenues.
❖ Boosting income with one-off gains.
❖ Moving current expenses to later, or earlier, periods.
❖ Failing to record liabilities or improperly reducing them.
❖ Shifting current revenue to a later period.
❖ Shifting future expenses to the current period as a special charge.

Nevertheless, as the recent corporate crises show, few boards appeared to be that awake or to care about the consequences.

In this chapter I am not going to focus on directoral corruption or bribery as corporate fraud; that was covered in Chapter 4. Here I want rather to examine the psychology of what happens when that group of big egos known as "the board" sit around the boardroom table to exercise their judgment on the appropriate policies, strategies, and controls to ensure a healthy, sustainable business.

A fundamental building block for any board is trust: trust in each other and being trusted by the owners and stakeholders. Trust is defined most simply as "having confidence" in oneself and in others. Directors need the assurance that they are all telling the truth, not working to a hidden agenda, and not having illegal or undeclared interests. They must be able to trust that once a decision is taken the other directors will stay committed to it outside the boardroom and be comfortable living with the consequences. A lack of trust, especially when big egos are involved, usually spells periods of great corporate uncertainty when the primacy of the board's fiduciary duty flies out of the window.

Trust is based on having confidence in another individual and in the legitimacy of their position, formal and psychological. Such legitimacy is made manifest in a person's exercise of their authority. This authority comes, according to the eminent sociologist Max Weber, from one of three roots: tradition, charisma, and rational process. In the modern world democracy is a strong, but not the only, rational process for the exercise of legitimate authority. The proven success of such industry-leading companies as Mercedes-Benz, Sony, and Microsoft gives them a form of rational, and generally accepted, legitimacy. Their obvious success is derived from meeting customer needs in the long term in a consistent manner and so creating a dominant market position. Psychologically speaking, they can continue to bank on their legitimacy provided that they are seen to be doing well over the long term. When things go wrong, as they will inevitably, they will usually be given a short-term respite by their customers to correct matters.

The eminent historian Francis Fukuyama's seminal book *Trust*[1] makes the point well: "Legitimate regimes have a fund of goodwill that excuses them from short-term mistakes." I would add, provided that they are seen to apologize and learn quickly from those mistakes. If not, you end up with the rapid demise of such a seemingly legitimate and rational institution as Andersen. Its disappearance globally within months is a fine example of the dangers of being seen as publicly illegitimate. How legitimate is your board?

The huge majority of boards are not venal. They do not set out to steal people's money, provide bad goods and services, or plan systematic fraud. Nevertheless, often they do set off on ill-considered, ego-boosting, and value-destroying strategies and whims. It is these unthought-through actions and their often dreadful consequences that do so much to destroy both shareholder value and, therefore, trust in boards and business. Given the present performance of most boards, it is hardly surprising that the public perception is that they are at best only semi-professional and so not to be trusted.

Sources of Personal Power

Before we can discuss abuses of power, we need to look at where that power resides. If we consider any board of directors sat around the boardroom table, it is quickly obvious that these individuals have very different characteristics, experiences, and even within themselves are complex mixes of sources of personal power. For the board to work effectively, it is essential for the chairman to identify and optimize such personal, directoral differences.

Both Revans[2] and Ashby[3] showed that any living organism needs sufficient variety within it to give it the ability to adapt continuously to its changing environment. Boards are no different. Yet throughout history most power players have a habit of choosing others who are like themselves and of pruning out differences, often ruthlessly. A board of "cloned" directors—same age, same sex, same professional background, same educational background, same social background—is usually ultra-friendly, under-powered, and as boring as hell. Over time it will ensure the death of any business.

That is why it is wise for the electing owners always to strive for directors with the healthiest and widest possible experience mix, both executives and outsiders, to optimize the board's direction-giving effectiveness. The managing director must never be allowed to pick his or her own board. It is the owner's job to select directors. With the pressure from the Myners' Report (see Chapter 2) for pension fund trustees to intervene in their under-performing investments, this will be taken much more seriously in future.

The key question for the chairman, and the responsibility of each director, is how best to deploy these crucial directoral personal power sources to achieve the company's purpose.

A comprehensive list of an individual's sources of personal power[4] must include:

- *Physical power*—their use of individual size, shape, physical prowess, and proximity.
- *Position power*—their formal job titles, responsibilities, and authority in the organization and consequent patronage opportunities.
- *Information power*—both through the formal organizational structure and the informal access and data that position can bring.
- *Expertise power*—the exercise of recognized competence that differentiates an individual director from others.
- *Connection power*—the social networking skills and use of informal connections: Who travels with whom to work? Who is in which clubs or societies?
- *Charismatic power*—a few directors radiate such charisma that many people will follow them regardless of the task or ethics employed.
- *Visionary power*—a few, very few, directors have such a clear and convincing picture of how the world will be in the distant future

that many people will go cheerfully with them toward that long-term end.

All of these sources of personal power are measurable for each director and need regular assessment as part of the annual board evaluation process. By sharing such personal measures openly within the board, and discussing the best ways in which they can be deployed to ensure effective group decision-taking, a lot of the "normal" board power issues drop away. Directors are encouraged to play to their strengths and their allowable weaknesses are acknowledged and compensated for. It takes time to build such trust among people with big egos, but openness does wonders for killing both self-doubt and self-delusion about personal power. Robert Burns' lines are a very useful reminder at board level:

Oh wad some Pow'r the giftie gie us
To see oursels as others see us!
It wad frae mony a blunder free us,
And foolish notion.[5]

This helps explain why regular board appraisal processes are beginning to make their appearance.

Uses of personal power

The personal and group scores on sources of personal power can drive a focus on optimizing the three strategic aspects of more effective board working, particularly the idea-generation, risk-assessment, and decision-taking processes relating to:

❖ Ideas (where are we going and why?)
❖ Content (how are we going to get there?)
❖ Information (what data will we work on?)

But much still depends on the directors' and board's specific needs for:

❖ Inclusion.
❖ Affection.
❖ Control.

It is paradoxical that, for example, many managing directors publicly express a great need to be a member of the board (inclusion), to be recognized for their individual contribution (affection), and to feel in charge (control); yet privately they often express a low need for inclusion, a low need for affection (even though it is nice to have, they feel they do not need it and may well not reciprocate it), and have no wish for anyone to control them at all (especially shareholders and even less stakeholders).

Such differences between directors' expressed and desired personal needs on the board make the chairman's job tricky, especially if there is an "achievement-greedy" managing director. So the challenge for the chairman is to achieve a positive balance between the development of the often paradoxical aspects of challenge and trust on the board. To do this effectively requires the chairman to counter power abuse by creating a positive learning environment across the whole board—the concept of the learning board (see Chapter 7).

The Abuse of Board Power

For the last two decades the media have rightly been stepping up their campaigns against incompetent and corrupt business people. However, these attacks have been highly generalized. To achieve focus and clarity I believe that we must return to considering the misunderstanding and abuse of power by the managing director or CEO, especially around the boardroom table. Its debilitating effect on board performance has rarely been considered in much detail. This is what I want to explore more deeply, having had the privilege of being invited frequently to observe, evaluate, and develop boards in action.

The ideals behind the three values of current corporate governance best practice—the previously mentioned accountability, probity, and transparency—are rooted firmly in the notion that people with an official position in the private, public, or not-for-profit sectors should not abuse their office. They should be paid sufficiently to do their job well without the temptation of bribery or greed, or the necessity to exploit their position to support their families or friends; a point made strongly in Singapore, which has the highest-paid government officials in the world and some of the lowest bribery and corruption levels. I am using corruption here to mean the *abuse of office for personal gain* and use this meaning throughout the chapter.

A return to the Corinthian Spirit?

What is the opposite of abuse of power? Is it possible to have honorable, professional directors who subscribe to the higher ideal that their primary loyalty is to the company as a separate legal entity and who will commit not to be self-serving? I believe that it is, and that the majority of directors are already there, or wish to be there. The problem is that they are often held back by one or two powerful personalities who are driving their own agendas at the expense of the company and its owners. How can one help such blocked, nonfunctioning directors reassert those values that they would like to hold dear? An explicit statement of board values, the commitment of each director to them, followed by a rigorous annual appraisal based in part on these values, are a good start along the road to the professionalization of boards.

The ancient Greek Corinthian ideal underpins the values of current professionalism and honest-dealing behavior. It energized and led the British Empire for two centuries by creating a truly disinterested administrative élite, developed through an approach to sport and life consciously generated in the fee-paying school system:

> As I understand the breed, he is one who has not merely braced his muscles and developed his endurance by the exercise of some great sport, but has, in the pursuit of exercise, learnt to control his anger, to be considerate to his fellow men, to take no mean advantage, to resent as a dishonour the very suspicion of trickery, to bear aloft a cheerful countenance under disappointment, and never to own himself defeated until the last breath is out of his body.
> Nick "Pa" Lane Jackson, *Sporting Days and Sporting Ways*, 1932

This is the antithesis of the Gordon Gecko creed later made manifest in the behavior of, for example, Merrill Lynch's internet analyst Henry Blodget, or Salomon analyst Jack Grubman who consistently gave high ratings to WorldCom stock. If I exchange the words "the pursuit of exercise" for "the pursuit of *excellence*," then from line three onward you have a very credible values statement for any director, and board, of a modern company.

Cynics may laugh that these are "old-fashioned" values. That is precisely what they are—and proud of it. Indeed, Peter Drucker reinforces the very point[6] that Britain's Indian Empire was run effectively by some 200 such young men—the District Officers—whose code was incorruptibility and well-honed self-effacement. They had, by today's standards, remarkably large areas of autonomy and discretion to suit the local conditions in their massive geographical territories. Each week they wrote three pages back to HQ in Delhi. One page was their analysis of the present situation. The second was their predictions of probable future developments, and the third page covered any other issues of which they thought the Viceroy should be aware. As Drucker points out, this was a remarkably effective, precise, and hugely cost-efficient system that worked well for some 200 years. It is still worthy of serious consideration by today's directors and senior executives.

The Three Fundamental Direction-giving Questions

If the abuse of power on the board is not regulated, preferably self-regulated, it is impossible for optimal decisions to be taken. The essence of these strategic decisions lays in three areas on which any board must be agreed:

❖ In which *direction* are we going?
❖ On which *ideas* are we working to get us there?
❖ On which *information sources* will we rely?

It is only when there is consensus on all three that there is a sporting chance of delivering the primary purpose of board work: driving the enterprise forward while keeping it under prudent control. But most directors are trained in neither and are, therefore, highly susceptible to being influenced by one or two powerful individuals who will bulldoze their own ideas and strategies through the board. What can be done to counter this?

The Chairman's Neutral Role

Power corrupts the few, whilst weakness corrupts the many.
Eric Hoofer, *The Passionate State of Mind*, 1954

If a camel gets his nose in a tent, his body will soon follow.
Arabic proverb

All boards are micro-political. It is human nature that a group of big egos is going to fight and try to "out-shape" each other, if only for the sport. This is where the psychological aspects of boardroom abuse cut in. If my research into UK boards' thinking styles is correct,[7] in a board of directors the large majority will start by being driven by the "soft" personal thinking styles of "gut feel," "sensing" (the immediate micro-political environment in and around the boardroom table), followed by strong "(post)-rationalizing" drivers. These will be used by the power players to ride roughshod over others' thinking styles of "values and commitments," valuing the "hard facts," and will especially deride the "ingenuity" needed to implement their strategy. This will ultimately spell disaster for any business because the board's psychological energies are then focused on fighting interpersonal politics rather than on the development of imaginative and implementable strategies—unless the directors can be trained to think and behave more constructively and collegially.

The interplay of the powerful personalities around a boardroom table will always need careful handling. This is the chairman's job, and it is a demanding one. While powerful personalities often enjoy controlling others, they do not enjoy being controlled themselves. Moreover, powerful personalities are rarely "team players," yet a board is legally collegial and must learn to operate at the very least as an effective workgroup on the occasions when it meets.

These two issues of board power and control processes affect directors' strategic thinking, group roles, leadership styles, and conflict-resolution processes. All of these are easily measurable, but rarely are. So boards often blunder around like short-sighted rhinoceroses, fighting their immediate, micro-political, and often banal battles while the outside world moves on, sidelining their business and allowing corrupt practices to evolve around the boardroom table. They will continue to make all issues personal unless they agree to raise their thinking and behavior to address such differences on a business level, rather than slugging it out in a one-to-one power battle.

An understanding of the law helps depersonalize many of the fights. The law in most countries demands that the directors elect a chairman—the "boss of the board"—who oversees fair play in the board's information-receiving, idea-generation, risk-assessment, and decision-making processes. The chairman is technically neutral and must declare his interest in the issues under discussion. Chairmen need training for their role, and at least annual assessment.

Very basic training in the processes of chairing a board will allow a chairman to umpire a board in a neutral manner. When his interests are in conflict, for example if he wishes to pursue a particular idea or strategy, he must declare the interest and relinquish the chair for that item, letting a director who is neutral on the subject chair that part of the meeting. This may sound strange, even wimpish, especially if you are fixated only on the "chairman as power-broker" mindset. Yet it works surprisingly well, provided that all directors adopt the collegial mindset with the chairman *primus inter pares*. It reinforces the three values of corporate governance because it allows a freer flow of accurate information (probity) and yet people can fight their corner. It encourages more diversity of thought, critical review, and risk assessment (transparency) in board decision-making and so allows more directoral commitment to policies, strategies, and executive results (accountability). This reduces the number of chances of "betting the company" on a chairman or managing director's pet obsessions.

Coping with psychological corruption

For a courageous chairman and board there are some very simple, practical ways of handling abuses of office. Such corruption is as much about psychological abuse as financial chicanery.

First, make the issue explicit to highlight any corrupt acts. In the *Guidelines for Corporate Governance* from the CACG,[8] Section 5 states: "Directors at all times have a duty to, and responsibility to, act honestly." It goes on:

> *A director should not obtain, attempt to obtain, or accept any bribe, secret commission or illegal inducement of any sort, and this should be actively discouraged throughout the organisation with appropriate sanctions where it is found to have taken place.*

In Section 7 the guidelines say: "The board should endeavour to ensure that the organisation is financially viable and properly managed." Explanatory notes stress how important it is that: "The personal interests of a director, or persons closely associated with a director, must not take precedence over those of the organisation and its shareholders."

It is easy for many current directors to treat both statements with cynical mirth. However, they are the basis of the key "probity" value of corporate governance and are likely to form an important part of the basis of future annual director appraisals. You do not have to set out to break immediately long-held cultural values to achieve noticeable improvement in this area. As we saw in Chapter 4, all you need do is to create a register of directors' interests, kept by the company or board secretary, updated frequently, and always open to inspection by the owners. At the start of each board meeting the chairman checks visually and verbally whether there are any conflicts of interests to be declared. These are recorded at the time in the minutes, together with a board decision on whether the director with that interest is allowed to debate and vote on the issue under discussion and why. The declarations and consequent decisions should be open to shareholder inspection at any time. This tends to concentrate directors' minds wonderfully, particularly as there is so much more criminal, rather than just civil, legislation developing in many countries to try and combat abuse of board power.

For many years there have been useful tools—particularly psychometric measures scoping the areas of thinking, role, leadership and development, and strengths deployment preferences—for analyzing what is occurring in power and influence terms in human groups. They are rarely applied to the board. Yet when they are they highlight easily what the dimensions of conflict are, and suggest what might be done about it.

Directors are rarely trained to handle the power dynamics within their own group. As access to what happens behind the boardroom door is so very difficult for outsiders, and as most boards want both the content and the processes of their decision-taking to be kept secret, research work in this area has been glacially slow. I argue that it should only be the content—the commercially sensitive information—that needs be closely held. The outline of the decision *processes* should be available for scrutiny and agreement by the owners (indeed, that is what the Turnbull Report on corporate governance demands of UK boards) and thus it should form part of the annual board appraisal system.

One of the biggest board conflicts occurs when the board and the chairman try to stop a managing director, or chief executive, pursuing a strategy that they think is doing harm to the company. Then the battle for board power and legitimacy is seen at its clearest. In the earlier corporate governance texts the central role of the board was given as "hiring and firing the chief executive." Things have moved a long way since then as the corporate governance movement has ensured that board roles and tasks are becoming better understood. But in the public's eye this fight to control the managing director is usually the one thing they think the board does.

The historical fight for overall power between the chairman and the managing director needs both to be addressed and resolved as the incumbents change. With the average life of a Fortune 500 CEO being three years and falling fast, this is a major issue. So I return to the legally correct, and very practical, notion that the chairman is the boss of the board, and the managing director is the boss of the daily operations of the company. If this is agreed between them, and accepted openly by the other directors, then many of the typical board power problems dissolve.

The board is designed as the balance mechanism, the regulator, to keep these two contradictory, centrifugal and centripetal, forces within it under reasonable and dynamic control. If any one force dominates for too long, the company will be in trouble. Too much enterprise and the business may well run out of cash and over-trade. Too little control and we lose the business; Barings, Marconi, Kirch, Vivendi, and Global Crossing are among many examples.

The law makes a heroic assumption here—that each director has the personal competence and the moral courage to uphold both of these aspects of the board's role while continuing to be "included" in the board. A powerful chairman or managing director can easily arrange the psychological exclusion of a director, unless there is a robust appraisal system to pick this up on behalf of the shareholders.

The problem of the actual or potential exclusion of a director was acknowledged in the UK's Cadbury Report of 1992, which recommends that an independent director must have access to external legal advice paid for by the company. This recommendation has been accepted by the more far-thinking boards. In addition, the law assumes that directors have a well-developed capacity of independent thought and critical review—and thus will be able to cope with the inevitable, and often abusive, power plays. This legal assumption is not proven.

Three Levels of Conflict in the Board

The development of a positive learning climate depends greatly on going more deeply, and openly, into a strengths deployment analysis[9] of the personal, and board, strengths, especially in the areas of:

❖ Assertion.
❖ Analysis.
❖ Nurturing.

Such an analysis looks at both what happens around the boardroom table when things are going well and, much more importantly, when things are going badly and business objectives are not being achieved. A map of these three personal and board strengths under positive and conflict conditions can be drawn up by the board for discussion and for benchmarking future personal and group development and appraisals.

One of the more interesting insights that frequently comes from such an analysis is that the strengths that have driven an executive up the career ladder do not always help him or her with the new board tasks. For example, a hard-driven sales director or finance director may be very strong in pushing for sales goals or analytical elegance respectively, but the strengths that got them to the board—assertion and direction-giving, or analytical autonomy—rarely ensure that they can function well as a full director. Indeed, it can quickly become very obvious that their driving strengths are soon seen by other directors as an obstacle to effective board working. For such driven people it takes some time, and careful coaching, to get them to a position in which they understand that their overdone strength will appear to others as a weakness.

If they can adapt to a full directoral role—and it often takes personal coaching by the chairman or external agents to rebalance their strengths—then they will become a valued member of the board. If not, as the inevitable conflicts occur they will adopt a mix of three decreasingly effective tactics to try to fight their way out of the problem. First, if the issue is seen as nonthreatening it will be avoided, joked off, or barked at loudly, with the hope that it will disappear. Humans are contradictory and they will habitually use first their biggest strength—assertion, analysis, or nurturing—in an attempt to get rid of the problem quickly.

If this does not work, we tend to fall back on our second highest strength to see if that will work. This "integrity-threatening" level of conflict is often harder to cope with, as we are falling back on a less used strength. If it is assertion we will not be quite so convincing; if analysis, we will find it harder to distance ourselves; if nurturing we will not sound quite so authentic. Nevertheless, we will usually get through the problem, if a little battered along the way.

The biggest issues come if neither of these two strengths works and we are thrown back on our final level of coping with conflict—the "last-ditch stand." Here we are using our least developed strength and if that is weak, the situation can become traumatic. If it is assertion, we will not be comfortable with ourselves and, in extreme circumstances, will resort to verbal or even physical violence. If it is analysis, we are likely to become highly reclusive and, in extreme circumstances, will pick up our toys and go home, removing ourselves entirely from the conflict. If it is nurturing, we are likely to feel very bad for some time about the fact that we cannot handle the other person or group better and, in extreme circumstances, that we have failed totally in our relations with other people. All of these three can lead to deeper psychological issues that require resolution.

Generating this confidential data both personally and for the whole board allows for directors' strengths to be appreciated and constructively deployed—but only if the members of the board have learned to trust each other. Then boards can be marvelous places to work and achieve good for both their business and society. However, if boards do not trust each other, a well-known set of problems emerges.

The Shadow Side of Boards

At what point does the interplay around the boardroom table stop being legitimate influencing of an idea or action and become degraded into bullying, harassment, discrimination, and the abuse of power? A simple answer is that this point has been reached when there is evidence that the majority of directors feel they cannot fulfill their legal roles and are consequently becoming depressed, have low morale, do not participate, and show signs of absenteeism, sickness, self-censorship, and under-performance.

Despite the popular myths, a great deal of such abuse comes not from one powerful person, but from collusion, implicit or explicit, among directors to avoid their differences, and so maintain the status quo regardless of the often negative impact on the company. This is a larger-scale version of the abuse of office for personal gain. Here we are talking about the abuse of office by the majority for short-term personal comfort. What is alarming is that such coercion does not have to be done *to* a director; it can be so easy for an individual to drift into a state of mind where they *self*-coerce. This can be post-rationalized by thinking that it is often more comfortable to do this because they don't want any conflict with their colleagues. Yet it then becomes increasingly difficult for directors to continue with their personal integrity intact.

Personal Integrity and Professionalism

This point about personal integrity is crucial. Rigorous independence of thought and action plus sticking to the ethic of "my word is my bond" is to be encouraged as a guiding principle for building trust around the boardroom table. It may be OK for actors to say "if you can fake sincerity, then you have it made," but this does not go for directors.

When the US Congressional hearings were underway after the Wall Street Crash of 1929, the senior partner of Deloittes was being questioned about the limits of the policing role of auditing. He was asked what the control mechanism was once the formal processes were exhausted. He replied: "My conscience." This demonstrates how far the ethical basis of professionalism has eroded since then. When I was trained in professionalism in the mid-1960s it was made crystal clear that we must always put our client's best interest before our own, even if it meant we lost out financially in the short term. Today may be the first time in over two decades that professionals are becoming willing to listen to such advice again, will try to live it, and will create an effective system of self-regulation. Without it we are leading ourselves a merry, and self-defeating, dance.

There are two main themes in the idea of professionalism. First is the application of sound theory in practice. This assumes that a professional will always ensure that best practice is used in pursuit of the client's interests, and any deviation must be explained. At the very worst a professional must always "fail safe" on the side of the client.

The professional is held personally and legally accountable for his or her advice. Second is the notion of acting professionally as legitimization of the person's role and status in society—back to the importance of living the values of a professional rather than merely being called one. Here I am much more interested in best practice and in reinforcing the demands for accountability to the client. Being an investment banker may have had great social prestige, but that palls rapidly now when some of their leaders are exposed as rigging the market for a few insiders. Who exactly were their "clients"? And to whom are they accountable? The courts will now decide.

Eight Sources of Errors in Board Strategic Decision-Taking

How do issues of personal integrity and professionalism relate directly to board thinking and action? Irving Janis has written extensively about this issue, especially in *Groupthink*,[10] and it is worth reviewing his research. His argument is that there are eight main sources of error by which any decision-making group, particularly direction-givers, can delude itself. These are caused by a mixture of:

❖ The illusion of invulnerability.
❖ Collective efforts to rationalize.
❖ Unquestioning belief in the board's inherent morality.
❖ Stereotyped views of rivals and enemies.
❖ Direct pressure on dissident board members.
❖ Self-censorship of deviations from apparent group consensus.
❖ A shared illusion of unanimity.
❖ The emergence of self-appointed "mind guards."

Any one of these can lead to underperformance if it goes unchallenged, but in combination (I argue three or more) they can become deadly for any board and their business. Each board will have some aspects of these, and indeed in tiny, homeopathic doses some can be seen as positive drivers and bonders—provided that all directors are aware of them and test their validity frequently.

It is worth considering each of these eight components of group-think in a little more detail, as I have found that they frequently encompass the main characteristics of dysfunctional boards.

The illusion of invulnerability

This phenomenon is well known in politics where, say, a successful second term for a government often leads it into risks and policies that will not have majority support even in its own party. This delusion is usually felt on boards where the company and the board have been around for a long time and things seem to be going well.

According to media allegations, British Telecom was a classic example of a board focusing on a gradual move into privatized operations while maintaining a mainly public-sector mindset. The erosion of its old and very comfortable position as a monopoly supplier by regulators determined to create competition in the industry, plus the astonishingly rapid development of new digital telecommunications technology, left it lagging behind the market. Its board's rate of learning was not equal to, or greater than, the rate of change in its external environment. When it finally tried to take radical action, it overdid things and pursued the seduction of dotcommery and the rush into overpayment for 3G (third-generation mobile telephone) licenses. Where were the intelligently naïve questions? Where was the board? Who had the courage to challenge the prevailing board mindset of "me too"?

Such problems can also happen to a new board fired up with enthusiasm. Vodafone and Marconi are classic examples of how to overblow matters through ill-considered strategy and timing. The illusion of invulnerability is said to be a characteristic of family companies but I rarely find this, at least for those companies that have survived beyond three generations. They have developed ways of learning to survive and grow; perhaps not as the textbooks recommend, but they are thriving nevertheless.

Collective efforts to rationalize

This happens when new, or different, information appears that threatens the status quo. Often group pressure is brought to bear quickly to diminish, or demean, data and warnings that might lead directors to have to reconsider seriously their policy or strategy assumptions. The sources and validity of new information are often rubbished so that the directors can return to a position of rationalized comfort in which they still feel good about their previous decisions.

This can be a particularly dangerous mindset when the previous proposition came from the managing director and is backed by long-incubated plans and data from the executive directors. If the nonexecutives do not have the courage or personal integrity to challenge the data and assumptions, there will be trouble ahead. If the executives then go also into "mind-guarding" mode (see below), they can lead the board severely astray. Warren Buffett puts it simply:

> *Once a company moves earnings from one period to another, operating shortfalls that occur thereafter require it to engage in further accounting maneuvers that must be even more "heroic." These can turn fudging into fraud.*

Unquestioning belief in the group's inherent morality

Such a belief relies on the common self-delusion that "people like us could not take a bad or immoral decision." Protected by the type of post-rationalization mentioned above, it is a surprisingly common symptom of dysfunctional boards. It is what many NGOs use as a major lever with which to attack business. They are sometimes right, as few businesses have any internal or external ethical audit of their board decisions. Most have never even heard of the Institute of Business Ethics.[11] However, I do find NGOs, not-for-profits, health provision groups, and housing associations just as liable to delude themselves in this way.

I have dealt recently with eminent consultant doctors who have abused their position and their staff to achieve illegal personal ends, academics who have defrauded their colleagues, and housing managers who have operated in a consciously corrupt manner over the awarding of building contracts, as well as managing directors who "doctored" the accounts. None of them thought what they were doing was fundamentally wrong. Most saw it as normal practice—"the way we do things round here." They are usually very shocked when it is pointed out that such actions are wrong, lacking in professionalism and personal integrity, illegal, and sometimes criminal. The shock is even greater if the courts then act against their personal wealth and liberty.

Stereotyped views of rivals and enemies

Stereotyping comes from a lack of sensitivity to the changing external environment coupled with a lack of respect for the competition. The truth is often only acknowledged too late—when the board cries "We was robbed!" as it loses a contract long assumed to be the company's by right. Stereotyping often also shows contempt, or lack of care, for customers. The visual and verbal images used of rivals by the board and executives and the adjectives attached to the competition in both casual and formal conversations can reinforce such misleading stereotypes.

For me the classic example is the end of the British Airways vs. Virgin Atlantic "dirty tricks" court case when Lord King, then chairman of BA, said: "I never imagined that we could be beaten by a man with a beard and a cardigan." Many boards demonize their opposition so that they can feel better about them. They stress their weaknesses and stereotype them as too evil or stupid to make any significant impression on the market. Such self-delusion is unhealthy and needs frequent doses of hard facts to counter it. Sadly, my research shows that people who become directors are often not that good at dealing with hard facts.

Direct pressure on dissenting directors

This is the oldest trick in the abuse-of-power book. A questioning director is subjected to ridicule, exclusion, and, especially, questions as to his or her loyalty to the board. Such pressure can be very distressing indeed. It is the chairman's job to protect such a director and to focus the questioning on the specific issue rather than the personality. The basic question is: "What is best for the future of the company rather than the immediate cohesion of the board?"

However, it is not unknown for a chairman to be the very person bringing the pressure to bear. So where does a dissenting director go then? The first answer is to the corporate rulebook and the company secretary. The latter has a duty to put on to an agenda any item the director wishes. The chairman and managing director do not have a legal right to edit the board agenda, although most directors do not seem to know this. Once the issue is on the agenda the views of the other directors can then be more directly addressed in relation to their fiduciary duty.

A director may want to seek external legal advice, and under UK best practice this is paid for by the company. If a mixture of his (or her) influencing skills and back-up legal advice is insufficient to sway his colleagues, then he must ensure that the disagreement is recorded fully in the board minutes. If the problem persists, he has to consider his position and, ultimately, resign. He could take his concerns to the shareholders, who can call an extraordinary general meeting or raise the issue at an AGM. Interestingly, in the proposed UK Company Law Review Bill it is suggested that at the resignation of any director of a listed company the outgoing director must give a written statement as to his or her reasons for resigning and this must be shown in the next annual report. That alone would make a huge difference to the abuse of power on boards.

Self-censorship of deviations from apparent group consensus

Self-censorship is often felt to be more insidious, and much more personally demeaning, than yielding to explicit group pressure to conform. It relies on individual directors not exercising their right to think and question freely. This means that they will withhold information or ideas, or deliberately not question proposals about which they have doubts, nor will they put up counterproposals.

Self-censorship is driven by such a strong set of intellectual and behavioral norms and group policing processes around the board that each director knows quickly what is and is not "discussable." They will be aware of what is "on message" or not and, regardless of the information or ideas they hold, will not put them forward for fear of being expelled from the board or ridiculed by it.

The shared illusion of unanimity

This is a natural consequence of the mixture of self-censorship, uncritical questioning, and review. It is made much worse by the common and convenient delusion that silence means assent. An overpowerful figure pushing for a specific decision and employing intellectual and behavioral bullying and harassment tactics will usually go down this path by merely forging on, not pausing for comment or questioning, until the logic of the proposal seems so irrefutable that no one can do anything but agree (or so he or she hopes). This approach often works in the short term (and many managing directors are only around for two years on average), but it can have terrible longer-term business consequences when the truth finally catches up—no one will admit that they supported the person concerned; indeed they will often actively denounce them.

Such behavior is well known in the psychological literature through the "Abilene paradox." This was a case about people sitting around on a hot and sticky summer's day when the wisest thing to do was nothing. However, one of the group suggested unenthusiastically that they drive 50 miles to the town of Abilene. Slowly but surely all agreed and they made the uncomfortable journey. When they arrived there was little to do, so they decided to eat and over lunch they found that none of them had wanted to go in the first place. It was just an idea to which they acquiesced without thought or critical review.

What is most alarming is that *boards are quite capable of taking decisions with which no director present agrees.* Unless the chairman tests agreement rigorously as a regular part of his chairing routine, this can lead down the path to eternal corporate damnation.

The emergence of self-appointed "mind guards"

Mind guards are members inside, and just outside, the board who consider it their duty to protect the board from information that they feel is prejudicial or adverse to board decisions, or that might shatter the board's solidarity about the effectiveness, efficiency, or morality of its decisions. Typical of these mind guards will be board members who see it as their role to be the monitor/evaluator of the discussability of board items: They will "sheepdog" difficult issues or facts until they are safely penned. This is true also of many board support staff—executives, personal assistants, consultants, and researchers are typical—who have their own agendas to protect.

Some of the most dramatic examples of things going wrong for boards have been in pharmaceutical companies where research results on new chemical entities are either suppressed before they reach the board or only partially given. Yet on these half-facts momentous strategic business decisions have been taken.

Janis's "symptoms of defective decision making" in *Groupthink* can also be used as a checklist by chairmen and directors in relation to any proposal put before a board. Are the proposals showing signs of:

❖ An incomplete survey of objectives?
❖ An incomplete survey of alternatives?
❖ A failure to examine risks of preferred choices?
❖ A failure to re-evaluate earlier rejected choices?
❖ A poor information search?
❖ A selective bias on processing information?
❖ A failure to produce contingency plans?

These will give directors a measurable reality check way beyond the easy assumptions and comfortable illusions of much of board life.

Professionalizing Board Performance

Boards were designed originally to ensure proper auditing and development of the company's primary purpose, vision, values, and performance. These primary needs must still be monitored and developed continuously for any board to be effective. Training and coaching the directors to competence—ensuring directoral knowledge, skills, and attitudes—then using and celebrating the diversity around the boardroom table is fundamental to this. Only then can the true power of a board be released. Working in such a group should be an enjoyable experience; after all, the word "company" derives from the Latin *companio*, with its association of people coming together in trust to break bread.

However, it must be remembered that the flesh is weak and humans will often yield to temptation or pressure. This tendency should never be forgotten by a board, and especially the chairman. Nor should the board's ability to set, wittingly or otherwise, the "emotional climate" of its total organization. These two ideas are brought together in business folklore through the famed story of the five monkeys:

A cage contained five monkeys. Hanging in the cage was a banana on a piece of string and under that was a ladder. A monkey would start to climb the ladder to reach the banana, but as soon as that happened the other monkeys would be sprayed with cold water by the experimenter. For a time other monkeys also tried to reach the banana, but always the remainder were sprayed with cold water. Soon the other monkeys tried to stop any of their peers trying to reach the banana.

Then the cold water treatment was stopped, one monkey was removed from the cage, and a new one introduced. As the new one went to reach the banana it found to its great surprise that the others stopped it quite viciously. Soon it learned that this would happen whenever it tried for the banana. Then another of the original monkeys was removed and replaced. The newcomer was attacked as soon as it tried for the banana and the previous newcomer joined in with gusto. Then the third, fourth, and fifth original monkeys were replaced in rotation. Every time a newcomer tried for the banana it was attacked, even though by now most of the attackers had no reason to know why they were doing this.

After replacing all of the original monkeys, none of the remaining monkeys would ever have been sprayed with cold water. However, no existing monkey would approach the ladder. Why? Because as far as they were concerned that was the way that things had always been done around there.

And that illustrates how both "board policy" and "company policy" can have disastrous consequences if applied uncritically.

Ways Forward

Much of the negativity described in this chapter can be countered through developing effective neutral chairing, rigorous board evaluation processes, decent directoral training and appraisal processes, and the declaration of interests of each director for each board item. I shall go into details in Chapter 8. In addition, the board must ensure rigorous and open internal and external audit processes.

The most effective managing director I have met developed a very professional, but arm's-length, relationship with the board's audit committee and a remarkably open relationship with his head of internal audit. He made sure that his behavior truly reinforced the message: "My door is always open to both of you." They built up such trust that the inevitable many minor infringements were nipped in the bud well before they turned into a board issue, rather than becoming festering sores or accepted ways of doing business. Because they never reached the board, they never caused a crisis for it. In addition, the managing director also accepted that the chairman must have a strong relationship with the head of the board's audit committee and that he should not attempt to influence them, or the external auditors, other than to explain his reasoning and seek their advice. Interestingly, this board has gone on to agree that it should pursue the "triple bottom line" approach and has instructed its internal and external auditors to ensure that they will measure all three dimensions annually.

Having dealt with the frailties of human nature, it is to more developmental attitudes and issues that we turn in the remaining chapters.

CHAPTER SIX

Directoral Dashboards

The New Board Metrics

W hile management accounts are commonly used, until now there has not been any serious focus on the idea of *director* accounts. On most boards there has therefore been an over-reliance on management numbers. This is hardly surprising, because if you only have a hammer most problems tend to look like nails. However, directors are not managers. They need to keep their eyes on a different pattern of figures, so they need a *directoral dashboard* to help them oversee total business performance.

If boards use only the old trio of balance sheet, profit and loss account, and management accounts, there is a tendency for them to be seduced into an easy fixation on micro-managing and cost-cutting (a necessary focus for executives in the business efficiency cycle, see Figure 3 in Chapter 4) rather than on future revenue generation (a necessary directoral focus relating to the changing external

---

This chapter is co-written with my colleague V "Ram" Ramakrishnan, Managing Director of Organisation Development Ltd, Singapore, whom I must thank for giving me access to his research work and extensive international business experience in Asia and Europe. His unique blend of analysis and practice has led to an exciting synthesis that points the directoral way ahead in understanding and measuring the unique board role of adding value for shareholders. He is focusing this knowledge on making explicit the board's balancing contribution to both the prudent control tasks of a board and its driving forward roles. He is linking these into assessing the effects of the board's policies and strategies on the business's total shareholder value added. His work is copyrighted. I take full responsibility for the editing of this chapter.

environment that delivers business effectiveness). The board's role is continuously to balance the pull between business effectiveness and business efficiency. Should they fail, they will get sucked into that well-known business decline spiral:

❖ Downsize.
❖ Rightsize.
❖ Dumbsize.
❖ Capsize.

The board's ultimate test of effective stewardship is adding shareholder value, demonstrated on the balance sheet. The executive's ultimate test of managing efficiency is made manifest in the profit and loss account.

Corporate Sustainability through Adding Shareholder Value

The definition of "shareholder value" that we find most useful (based on Sir Brian Pitman's work) is:

> *Shareholder value is the surplus of economic value after satisfying all reasonable short-term stakeholder expectations, taking into account the cost of capital, and after providing for the long-term health and security of the business.*

This spans both shareholder and stakeholder aspects, and the board conformance and board performance aspects. Indeed, we argue that it *defines* the board performance aspect.

The easy directoral chant that it is the board's job to add value to the business is made with increasing regularity, but often with little realization of its implications. The last decade's business wisdom was that in simply ramping up the share price, to the immediate benefit of short-term investors, speculators, and executive stock options but to the detriment of the shareholders' long-term interests, the managing director and the board were doing their job.

A typical example would be Walt Disney, where the board left the CEO strictly alone as the revenue grew strongly and the share price rose excitingly. However, come the denouement and the board's final intervention, there were acrimonious departures of top executives.

There is an argument that ultimately there can only ever be short-term interests (because without them there is no long term) and, therefore, no other sentiment can stand in the way of the immediate operation of the markets. This is a counsel of despair, lacking the human drive of vision, strategic imagination, the opportunities for the long-term funding of enterprise, and any sustained commitment to the board's fiduciary duty of continuing the creation of sustainable wealth for the owners and stakeholders.

However, the majority of boards still tend to be so profit centric and share-price centric that a set of frequently disconnected numbers has been used to create the illusion of business progress. The illusion is sustained by increasingly complex software that can capture and mine such data, often without the realization that garbage in still gives garbage out, especially on the revenue-generation side. Costs seem much easier to track, but have proved as easy for directors to confuse, manipulate, and over-do as the revenue streams. It is a rare and often unpopular director who persistently questions the source of value capture and the utilization of assets in delivering value.

Our argument is that rigorous and regular measurement of share-holder value as defined above delivers fiduciary duty by raising the board's intellectual perspective and thinking competences well above both those of the executive role and the purely financial perspective. We must, therefore, find ways of tracking and measuring the board's inputs and outputs at this more strategic level.

There are three operational problems with the shareholder value concept. First, how practically do you measure the added shareholder value? Second, how can you then assess the contribution that the board, and even individual directors, are making to this? Third, how do you separate the contribution from the executive team as distinct from the board? These questions are as old as the very concept of joint-stock companies, with their mutually agreed risk-taking and rewards, yet they still have no easy answer.

Nevertheless, they are worth pursuing. The Stern Stewart consultancy is justly renowned for its development of the notion of Economic Value Added™ (EVA), calculated by measuring the difference between the company's net operating profit after tax (allowing for agreed adjustments of its reported numbers) and its capital charge (calculated by multiplying capital employed by the cost of its capital). This gives a very good view of whether the company is creating shareholder value, and at what rate.

Following the dotbomb failures, the rise of EBITDA (earnings before interest, taxes, depreciation, and amortization) as a debatable accounting measure, and the accounting and fraud scandals of the early 2000s, Stern Stewart has developed a complementary index to measure total corporate performance from the *shareholder* viewpoint—the Wealth Added Index™ (WAI). This assesses the company's return on equity against the cost of equity, using the capital asset pricing model (the basis of much modern portfolio theory and practice). So while EVA is based on the reported accounts, WAI is based purely on the performance of the share price. Given what was said above about both the nature of accounts and share prices, one still has to issue a caveat in using either tool. However, they have proved more effective than most and are worthy of investigation.

Recent results from Stern Stewart using the WAI model make interesting reading. Companies creating most wealth in the last five years (December 2001 base, in $million) include:

	WAI
WalMart Stores	149,662
Microsoft	93,780
IBM	93,032
General Electric	91,857
Nokia	82,156
Johnson & Johnson	56,017
Nestlé	34,609
Royal Bank of Scotland	29,114
Shell Transport and Trading	24,792
HSBC	20,765

And those companies that have destroyed most wealth valued by WAI include:

Vodafone Airtouch	−104,574
NTT	−90,861
Lucent	−86,594
Coca Cola	−68,211
Motorola	−40,781
Deutsche Telecom	−39,868
Compaq	−29,561
British Telecommunications	−21,214
Roche	−18,284
Singapore Telecom	−17,939

Given the huge range between the best and the worst companies over this five-year period, one can see the need for directors to get to grips with the notion of measuring value creation and the consequent performance of boards.

Directoral Dashboards

We suggest an approach that Ram is taking with our clients in East and South Asia, after his earlier work in Europe. This develops the idea of "directoral dashboards" to measure the performance of both the board and the total business. The thinking is that we must develop systems that show graphically the performance of the company and its subunits in such a way that the board can monitor and understand its value-adding trend lines, and can measure these against their strategies, without feeling the need to intervene immediately in the operations of the business to correct matters.

The dashboard concept helps the board focus its attention on key business performance indicators, prioritizes the actions needed to be taken by the executives to implement strategies, and learns from their consequent effects, while also highlighting the consequences of not taking corrective action. Using a medical analogy, even a fledgling doctor can start an effective diagnosis if he or she has accurate basic data on the patient's pulse, heartbeat, eyes, pain, and quality of waste—and is taught from the start to hit the panic button if the patient's pulse is falling.

The directoral dashboard gives an index of board effectiveness in delivering short- and long-term profitability and added value—with cashflow as the panic button. It is for the executives alone to make the necessary managerial interventions, not the board. The board must create internal governance measures for the executives. It is they who provide the *conformance* aspects of the board's requirements—those hopefully rising trends showing that the operational objectives are being met or exceeded—while the board concentrates its major efforts on providing the *performance* aspects.

While the notions of "balanced scorecards" and "corporate dashboards" have been around for a decade or more, Ram's work has synthesized the ideas into novel, pragmatic board development tools. If we look at a car's dashboard, we see three critical dials: a speedometer to assess the speed at which the car is traveling, an odometer to measure the miles covered, and a fuel gauge to let us know how long in terms of time and distance we have before we need to refuel. Using a crude business analysis, if the business's "engine" is running in synchronization with its forward motion, the speedometer and odometer can be seen as the overall business achievement, covering the miles needed to achieve its goals and thereby adding value. The fuel gauge can be seen as measuring the cashflow through which the business remains alive. If the meters do not show synchronous running, the directors must take action before the corporate engine stalls.

Before we stretch this simple metaphor too far, let us remember what we said at the start: We are setting our directoral dashboards in the broader context of the board's role in seeking shareholder value, and the key risk/reward ratio that is so often missed when corporate measures are being discussed. The crucial assumption here is that the final measurement must be made against the cost of capital employed in the wealth-creating process. There is a varying threshold, unique to each business, at which profits start to contribute to value.

The fundamental measure of shareholder value is a balance of the cost of capital against the sum of the efficiencies of inputs on the operations side and the effectiveness of their outputs. The key question for investors and pension fund trustees is whether the board understands the value-creation process, the risk factors embedded in the drivers of such value creation, and the company's specific threshold.

The Primacy of Revenue Generation

Ram's international experience is that most boards appear lost when pushed to explain which factors, especially the key drivers and critical enablers, make their shareholder value threshold most sensitive. Many see just "dead" cost numbers and so demand more, or less, of the same as a knee-jerk reaction. They rarely budget the time, or have the intellectual inclination, to understand that future revenue generation is as important as cost management and managing productivity. Indeed, we would argue that it is more so.

The directoral dashboard focuses the entire board on the need to track the threshold-level indicators of financial performance and so to understand the key drivers and enablers that give business sustainability.

The main changes in directoral mindset needed to use the directoral dashboard idea effectively are a series of shifts in focus by the whole board:

❖ Away from a short-term, cost-oriented perspective to the sustained delivery of shareholder expectations.

❖ Away from an over-fixation on corporate governance compliance to a bias toward measured (and measurable) board performance.

❖ Away from an executive focus on short-term operational performance to a board focus on the long-term vitality of shareholder value performance.

❖ Away from a fixation on 12-month, and even quarterly, budgets to agreed longer-term measures of continuous incremental increase in shareholder value.

❖ Away from fixating on what drives the business to clarity on what enables the delivery of shareholder value.

❖ Away from seeing the business as a series of static snapshots to observing the dynamic, moving picture of the living business.

There are two main messages. First, if the board is too concerned with the short term, especially budgets focusing only on the enablers, it will lose focus on its main job of giving direction—ensuring vitality to the business drivers. Second, if the business is seen to be doing well in the short term this does not imply that it can develop in the longer term. Short-term profitability alone is necessary, but not sufficient, to deliver the board's fiduciary duty.

Recent studies of Economic Value Added, such as Stern Stewart's, have found a profound misunderstanding on the part of many directors and executives that merely producing a profit after tax implies good corporate health. They failed to grasp the depths to which the concept of added value should reach even within their own business, or its applicability. In Ram's experience the guardians of the accounting holy grail, the chartered accountants, are startled by the range of business operations that are affected by this simple idea, and the breadth of thinking styles needed by executives to benefit from it.

Many directors still believe that conforming to budgets is a sign that the business is adding value. In a fast-changing world sticking rigidly to a 12-month budget can have dire consequences. There is no law that budgets have to last for 12 months, except for poor farmers dependent on the seasonal rains—and even they have to contend with disruptions like El Niño. The board and executives therefore need to agree on a process where the timespan of the budget (the internal battle for scarce resources and consequent power) for each different business unit is agreed, then reviewed frequently and recast as necessary in the light of changing market conditions to meet the *strategic* objectives. If these strategic objectives need to be reviewed, that is fine— just remember to recalculate the cascading consequences down through the business.

This "action budgeting" process alone changes the quality of discussions between the board and the executives, and their subsequent planning and strategy-implementation processes. A successful example of this is the Swedish financial group Handelsbanken, which has run variable-time budgets successfully for at least 12 years. Many businesses become so myopically "budget fixated" that they lose the wider perspective in relation to market changes and so miss the beauty, drama, and challenges of their own business.

Value Added and Corporate Health

The value-added notion of "corporate health" requires that the board's focus is on "real-time coherence," cogently assessing and balancing the impact on internal factors of changes in the external environment as they occur. Generating strategic coherence—the opposite of strategic incompetence—is the heartbeat of Ram's model. The directoral dashboard focuses on the board's quantifiable and organizational goals and the rigorous discipline that this entails. Board goals must be deliverable—i.e., the strategies must be implementable—sustainable, and in line with shareholder expectations.

A good example of this latter point is Shell's use of triple bottom line reporting, discussed in Chapter 4. Here three annual audits are carried out by three independent auditors on the financial bottom line, the physical environmental usage (and abusage) bottom line, and the corporate social responsibility bottom line. As these go way beyond the normal remit of financial, figures-only auditing, they can be seen to take in the wider policy-formulation and strategic thinking aspects of true board performance. They are numbers focused, but not numbers fixated. The numbers are only enablers to understand trends, and patterns, within specific corporate policy themes. These are the keys to the true business drivers.

The directoral dashboard is designed to capture those few, vital measures needed to judge the *effectiveness* of total business performance. These are not the same measures that the executives use for their detailed assessments of operational *efficiency*.

The famous "seven ratios and twelve trend lines" of the late Lord Weinstock have been used widely by many boards:

Ratios

1	$\dfrac{\text{Profit}}{\text{Sales}}$	4	$\dfrac{\text{Sales}}{\text{Inventories}}$
2	$\dfrac{\text{Sales}}{\text{Capital employed}}$	5	$\dfrac{\text{Sales}}{\text{Debtors}}$
3	$\dfrac{\text{Profit}}{\text{Capital employed}}$	6	$\dfrac{\text{Sales}}{\text{No. of employees}}$

7 Sales per £ of emoluments

Trend lines

1	Sales	9	Trade debtors
2	Orders received	10	No. of employees
3	Orders in hand		Direct
4	Net profit		Indirect
5	Direct wages	11	Average wages per hour of direct labor
6	Overhead spend		Basic
7	Capital employed		Premium rates
8	Stock levels	12	Export sales (from total sales)

In the 1970s these were an early, and crude, start to the notion of corporate dashboards. While still hailed by many as the basic business financial discipline, they reflect only manufacturing industry and measure only the operational aspects of business performance. They are noticeably silent on the sustainability of revenue, and reflect the notions of steady growth in expanding economies.

Such ratios and trend lines are still useful executive data, but they have led too many boards to focus all their energies on studying minutely each cost "tree," while failing to see the forest of opportunities for revenue generation. They do not allow the board to review the impact of its policy or strategy on either the business's drivers or its enablers.

A rather later version was the famed Dupont pyramid (see Figure 4).

This classical pyramid approach was an example of taking a rigorous analytical approach to the evaluation of business performance. It is still valid as a basic operational overview of the total business. However, it does not take all the efficiency measures into account, nor does it attempt to grapple with the issue of assessing directors' performance through their judgments on strategies and risks. Historically, it is an important milestone in the assessment of performance dashboards because it introduces the idea of all the "numbers" being linked within the corporate ecosystem, where each set of figures supports its neighboring sets.

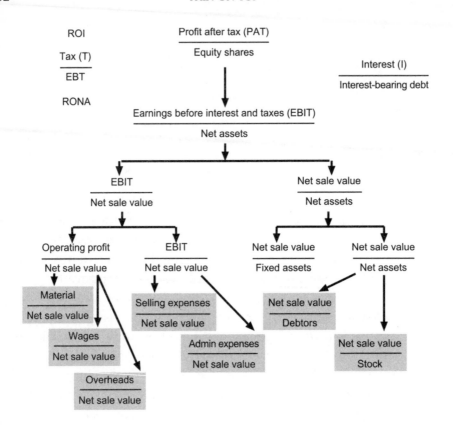

Figure 4 The Dupont pyramid of ratios

Directoral Dashboards and Board Learning

The directoral dashboard deliberately does not show all the executive numbers. It shows only the key results and trends of a deeper series of complex activities within the operational processes of the business as they affect achievement of the strategic objectives. Using the car analogy again, it does not show the details of the precise state of the engine, the transmission, suspension, electrical systems, or air pressure in each tire—these are the executive functions.

Ram and I are experimenting with a system that takes as read the detailed engineering of the vehicle at any one time—it is for the directors to ensure that such systems exist—yet still provides a reliable indicator of the health of the whole. When used well by "learning boards" (see Chapter 7), such dashboards allow a "missed beat" in the business engine to be rapidly seen and, by showing the executives where to "drill down" into the detailed figures, enables rapid correction of the problem before the whole engine stalls.

To benefit fully, the board, and executives, need to map their strategies. This is done through a "root cause" or "cause-and-effect" diagram that captures the linkages between the strategic objectives, drivers, and enablers. Everyone in the organization can refer to this map to understand how their work fits in, and will then be able to evaluate the impact of any deviation from plan on their work and the total system. This clear line-of-sight approach builds confidence and responsiveness across the whole business, and so gives the energy to move forward without continually looking over your shoulder to find out whether what you are doing is right. It gives the confidence to accept the system as a given so that creative energies can be focused on creating a healthy future for the firm.

We are field testing the process (Ram has several "beta sites" currently) to create a reliable system of board measurement that is not subverted as soon as there are signs of trouble. Our clients understand that this is a crucial asset and mindset and it has proved even more valuable in a crisis.

Facing up to Difficult Figures

One of the big corporate governance issues at present is executives' knee-jerk reaction of quickly burying any "difficult" figures or trends without warning the board. We have to design a "transparent" system where it is possible for directors to, as one of our clients calls it, "quickly hear their baby cry," and then be able to ask intelligently naïve questions of their executives that allow them, in turn, to drill down into any part of the system if that is necessary to reveal the accurate figures. Directors need a framework for better "forensic accounting." At the same time, the board must have confidence in the probity of their executives so that such board interventions happen only in a crisis. As we have said before, boards must not try to micro-manage their businesses from the boardroom.

We have seen the negative consequences of not installing such a transparent system—undue opacity, unethical behavior, and lack of accountability—with such examples as WorldCom, Inno-Pac, Enron, Adelphia, HIH, Swissair, and ABB.

It is noticeable that a lack of accountability seems to go hand in hand with poor ethical behavior, and that the latter is made transparent usually in embarrassingly difficult circumstances.

Barriers to Board Performance

To add sustainable shareholder value, the board's performance needs to be focused on the sustained delivery of shareholder expectations. However, these have frequently been dashed in the recent past by well-meaning, yet ill-founded, mainly political initiatives that have led to shareholder and public disillusionment in three main areas.

First, the over-regulation of boards through the generation of more and more laws, civil and criminal, when the rigorous imposition of existing laws would be sufficient to concentrate all directors' minds. Instead, many boards have adopted a "tick box," merely legislation-compliant approach, linked to a transfer of their energy into finding ways round the new laws, rather than focusing on driving the business forward.

Second, the nonlegislative ideal of board "self-regulation" demands a heroic assumption regarding the nature, integrity, and ethics of the people who become senior executives and directors, and their ability to take a true "helicopter view" of their business. At present the ideal is a long way from reality as so few boards are trained to professional competence. Cynics will say that this is using a fox to save the chickens. Yet we believe that board self-regulation is the golden mean at which we should all aim to ensure professional board oversight of the executives' actions. We view directoral dashboards as providing snapshots of the main and connected issues that will have a material impact on the sustained delivery of shareholders' expectations, and so improve the board's professionalism.

That leaves us with the third condition where, using another of Ram's metaphors, a dynamic balance is frequently struck between three opposing forces: the board (the legislature), the managers (the executive), and the regulators (the judiciary). The regulator will rarely have the same quality of access and information as the other two, yet must ultimately sit in judgment on them. This ideal is based on the learning board model, which, as will be discussed in Chapter 7, gives the four basic board tasks needed to ensure the directoral balance between board conformance and board performance:

- ❖ Policy formulation/foresight.
- ❖ Strategic thinking.
- ❖ Supervising management.
- ❖ Accountability,

One way of looking at this is to see that board performance is based on the pact agreed between the board and the managing director—it is based on the *ability to ask the right questions*. Board conformance is the pact agreed between the managing director and the executives to implement board policies and strategies while ensuring legal and financial compliance—it is based on the *ability to give the right (honest) answers*.

Any flashing light on the board's dashboard will be helpful in triggering a quick check by the (executive) mechanics before medium-term erosion of the business sets in. An effectively installed directoral dashboard gives the directors the ability to drill down into that executive structure to understand better how to question the executives on their operational, and planning, activities, while simultaneously maintaining the board's wider helicopter view.

Behind this thinking lies Ram's simple axiom that for shareholders the sustained delivery of expectations means satisfaction; and this is derived from actual performance less expectations:

$$S = P - EX$$

Before we get into the detail of how to construct a board dashboard, it is important to understand two other parameters that must shape the board's thinking in terms of its own performance, as described in Figure 5:

❖ Goal attainment—the primary driver.
❖ Resource utilization—the primary enabler.

DRIVERS

Market potential

Organizational potential

Organizational capability

Market capability

GOAL

Financial performance

ENABLERS

Financial performance

Organizational processes

Customer management

Continuous learning and innovation

Figure 5 Developing sustainable performance goals

Measuring Total Board Performance and Effectiveness

With these two parameters in mind, it is possible to construct a two-way flowchart based on my earlier work in developing strategic thinking, as in Figure 6.

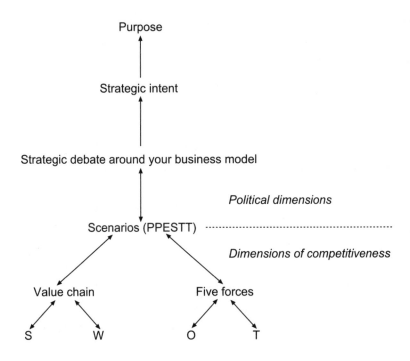

Figure 6 Developing strategic thinking

This flows from the board's highest levels of thinking and learning about policy formulation and foresight, through strategic thinking and the value propositions down into the detailed work of developing value chains, then drilling down into the necessary revenue growth and productivity into the detailed planning work derived from the strategy map and into the executives' own dashboard, with its performance measures on both development of the business and implementation of the strategy. Here we are deliberately balancing the board members' thinking with learning from their actions. The board is using its dashboard while the executives are doing the system checks and taking any reengineering actions necessary.

A way of clarifying this process is for directors to think of it in sequential terms from the board's viewpoint as (see Figure 7):

❖ Strategy development.
❖ Strategy translation.
❖ Strategy deployment and feedback.

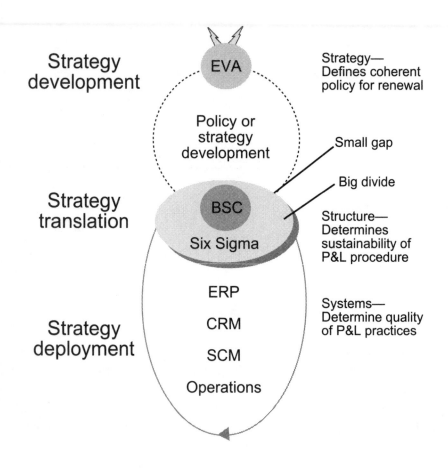

Figure 7 Strategic coherence

Collecting the Hard Data for the Dashboard

All of this leads us on to the process of collecting hard data—quantifying strategy and its results. This starts with the careful analysis of the business's key qualifiers—the core competences and operational strengths—that form the basis of that much-derided but very useful tool, the SWOT analysis (on which more in Chapter 7). The key qualifiers determine especially the strengths and weaknesses side of the SWOT. Then a tool such as the five forces model can help generate the value propositions that, coupled with scenario-thinking processes to give sensitivity to the rapidly changing external competitive environment, help frame the strategies needed to ensure effective customer management and corporate social responsibility.

It is then that the ideas created around the boardroom table, the rigorous debate over risk assessments, and the consequent board strategic decisions that deliver the added value from the board come into their own. Figure 8 shows the "value diamond" flowing from this process.

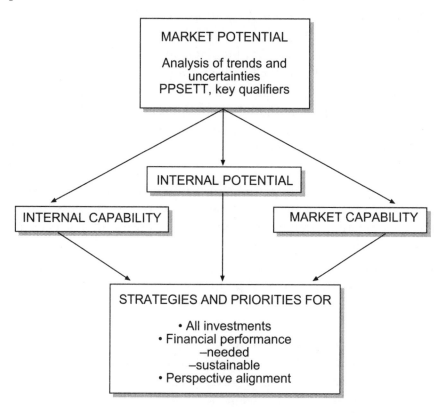

Figure 8 The value diamond

One can then construct a board development and control system that is robustly authentic at all levels of the business. The hierarchy of board information would be:

❖ Essential corporate information.
❖ Essential board information.
❖ Essential director information.

Constructing the Detailed Directoral Dashboard

The dashboard starts by identifying those external drivers that will give future revenue generation. By definition, many of these will be uncontrollable by the board; its members cannot by themselves alter political policies, demographic trends, climate changes, etc. However, they can become very sensitized to them and quantify them in such a way that they can be tracked continuously. This gives the board the space within which it can maneuver strategically. From this is derived the enabler concepts—both those that are necessary and those that are "nice to have"—that will deliver shareholder value.

So the dashboard identifies, measures, and reports on the difference between the potential of the markets and the business's delivery in those markets. Directoral dashboards capture and report the disequilibrium between the needed forward speed of the business and its complex internal support mechanisms—its organizational capabilities. That brings us back to the $S = P - EX$ formula. While both satisfaction and expectation are inherently intangible, and subject therefore to relative measures, performance must be explicit. It is the crucial measure of what gives sustainable competitive advantage. It is about finding out what the competition does not know and then building a key advantage with it.

As Clive Morton has shown, "world-class" companies[1] deliver continuous customer and shareholder satisfaction day in and day out, year in and year out, while using assets effectively, i.e., well beyond the costs used to acquire them. Insiders will tell you of the large quantities of analysis required at all levels of the organization to sustain world-class performance. Directoral dashboards help directors to focus on the complex sets of external and internal relationships and to express each element and its linkages clearly and logically.

This has the great advantage of making it much more difficult for executives to fudge the books. They may be able to do this once or twice, but the resulting discrepancies shown by "blips" in the trend lines will lead to the board automatically cross-examining the executives and, hopefully, exposing any "tangled web" with which they hoped to deceive.

Such questioning helps the board and the executives focus on the difference between "core business processes" and "core competences." While the efficiency of core processes is necessary, sufficiency comes from consciously developing specific core competences for the business. Again, we are back here to those few key differentiators from the competition, that complex mix of attitudes, knowledge and skills, know-how and know-why, and trade secrets that defines your enterprise.

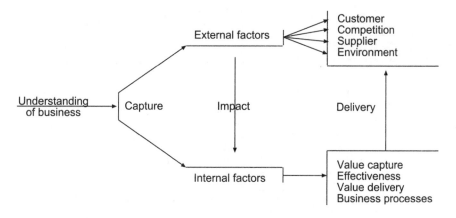

Figure 9 Developing practical strategy

This may look simple, commonsensical, even simplistic. However, in our experience common sense is quite rare around the boardroom table. It is unwise to assume that all directors and executives have even these basics internalized, understood, and committed to. It is

much wiser to assume, as many outstanding boards do, that it is key
to the board's prudent control role to question these basics regularly
and rigorously. It is this powerful mixture of understanding the basics
and yet seeing the complexities of the business's linkages, that allows
the board to know the correct levers to pull when there is trouble.
More importantly, unlike most boards, those using directoral dashboards can be assured that the enablers are actually connected.
Dashboards "pull" board performance.

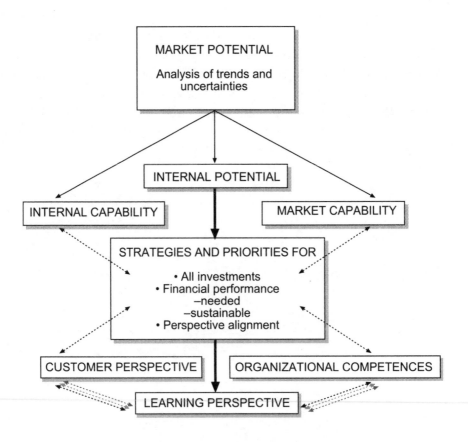

Figure 10 The corporate ecosystem

The directors need to understand their opportunities and capabilities in the markets, and to be able to match those with the internal competences (or acquire the necessary resources) *before* moving into their strategic risk and decision-taking cycle. Our experience is that because so many directors' thinking is driven primarily by "gut feel," they are surprisingly comfortable starting with little tested hard information and then struggling to deliver sustained value added. For them "real" strategic thinking starts only after the crisis hits. The "value diamond" suggests strongly that a continuous environmental scanning process is an essential prerequisite to delivering sustained shareholder value.

The directoral dashboard plots these trends as they affect the business so that the *variability* of tangible performance can be reduced. This helps see the forest rather than just the trees.

We stress again that while determining the appropriate dashboard metrics, it is essential that the board's system has the ability both to monitor customer and shareholder expectations, using the internal business measures, and to compare them with what is organizationally possible. This may seem to be the same as standard strategic gap analysis, but a well-designed system will ensure the sensitivity of the analysis of value delivery, and then determine how much value the business is ready to capture. The critical difference is that the directors can take corrective action in real time based on the actual performance gap versus the notional element in the strategic gap analysis model.

This means that substantial sensitivity analysis precedes exploration of the primary enablers, especially the ability to sustain delivery. From experience, a typical multiproduct business has between three and four key enablers. Smaller businesses tend to have just one or two. They make up by being nimbler, but their access to resources is lower. In all businesses getting the business initially can be as much chance as cause, but keeping the customer demands sustained delivery of customer satisfaction that will stretch all the enablers.

This is where the concept of the learning organization[2] is so important for a board to understand and aspire to. Reaching the happy state when all levels of the organization are learning in real time from improving their own jobs, and the linkages between them, is the goal of all boards and executives. Regular codification and interpretation of the dashboard figures help in the board's continuous learning.

An Example of Learning through the Directoral Dashboard

Let us take just one indicator of added shareholder value—economic value—as an example. The primary flows of economic value are:

❖ Growth in revenue.
❖ Lower costs through improvement in productivity.
❖ Better capital and asset utilization.

The three are closely intermeshed.

An effective dashboard design will establish the primary external drivers of each of these three. For example, revenue growth is market determined. The strategic choice of enlarging your market share is available, but depends on your ability both to generate funds and to acquire the organizational capability for this. Such an investment could reduce capital productivity while increasing costs. The board is paid to decide at which point expansion is viable, and beyond which it risks decreasing shareholder value.

Having established this, the key enabler discussion then focuses on whether the organization is capable of attracting, retaining, and developing the customer. Will the order pipeline be strong enough to justify the revenue growth? This can be a disconcerting type of question for many boards, who are more used to discussing cost-cutting measures, a much easier monster to slay. Then, what is the cost of capturing such a customer? Will the cash generated be sufficient to ensure a flow-through to added shareholder value? Therefore, will the capital employed be used effectively? Most boards do not have integrated systems that can show this rapidly.

If revenue growth can be sustained at a reasonable cost, then the five strategic decision options that will be discussed in Chapter 7 come into play. Where, and how, will the board ask the executives to advance, retreat, defend, hold, or surrender? Ram has developed a structured set of "doodle sheets" to guide the necessary thinking process and, most importantly, to provide a framework that helps ensure that the process is dynamic and continuous.

The Number of Dials on a Dashboard

How many dials should there be on a directoral dashboard? Given that the main dial will concern the resulting added shareholder value, then from experience we believe that between seven and ten dials are needed to have a reasonable chance of assessing the opportunities, risks, and costs involved in taking a strategic decision. Figure 11 shows the layout we prefer.

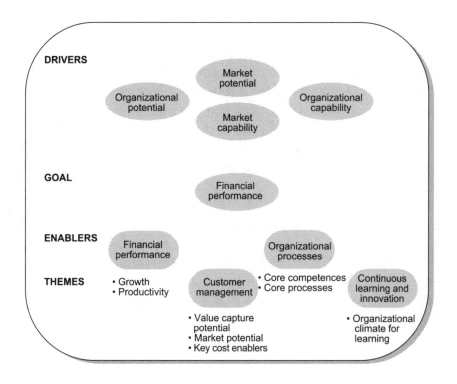

Figure 11 Dashboard layout for sustained value creation

For the economic value added example above, the nine dials (currently used by a client) indicate:

❖ Market potential.
❖ Market capability.
❖ Organizational potential.
❖ Organizational capability.
❖ Financial performance.
❖ Organizational processes.
❖ Customer management.
❖ Continuous learning and innovation.

Some of these drivers may need more than one indicator. This is the board's decision. The aim is to improve significantly the quality of insights that they give for the board's risk assessment and decision-taking. The deep learning for the board is to begin to understand the linkage of these indicators for its business. As this develops, so does the directors' ability to pull the appropriate lever quickly to trigger the right enabler, which then reinforces the right driver. This leads to the development of a "root cause diagram" (Figure 12).

This is a generalized root cause diagram that can be applied to most value-adding activities. Keeping it simple allows a board to focus intently on learning the essentials for keeping, and developing, its customers profitably—and to ensure that its executives have the same mindset.

The directoral dashboard can use most available strategic analysis tools. The trick is to employ them in such combination that the board learns the key linkages and understands their impact on each of the factors shown in the root cause diagram. Then boards can refine their SWOTs as the center of their strategic risk-assessing and decision-taking process. Ram argues that the job of directors is to improve their SWOT ahead of market requirements, and has developed a scoring system to guide directors in monitoring their own performance.

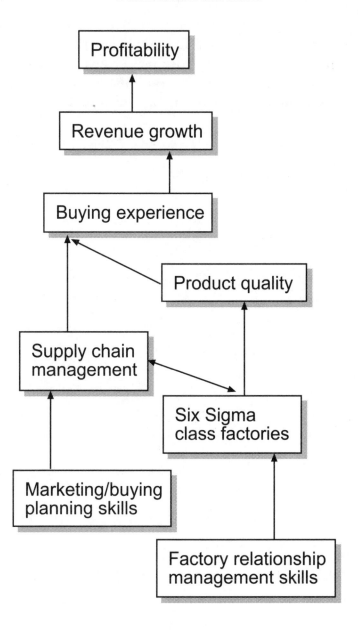

Figure 12 Root cause diagram

A well-used directoral dashboard can ruin any managing director's hopes of ramping up the share price for personal gain without the consequences being noticed by the board, long before the shareholders begin to ask tricky questions about the nature of their added value.

It is to learning and effective decision-making that we turn in Chapter 7.

CHAPTER SEVEN

Developing the Learning Board

The test of a first-rate intelligence is the ability to hold two oppos-
ing ideas in the mind at the same time, and still retain the ability to
function.

F Scott Fitzgerald, *The Crack Up*, 1936

MANY BOARDS' STRATEGIC DECISION-MAKING PROCESSES are weak, indeed some do not seem to have any definable *board* processes at all. Those that do exist are usually the sum of the output of warring executives, with little directoral input. The future for which the board must be giving direction is uncertain and full of ambiguity and complexity. Most directors do not have Fitzgerald's "first-class intelligence"; most are average human beings. Many are scared and confused by the idea of having to cope with uncertainty and instead crave certainty. So often only one solution, usually the managing director's, is proposed for the board's strategic discussion; and it does not take more than two brain cells for most directors to work out that it is likely to be a career-threatening move to challenge in any substantial way what is being "debated." This leads frequently to suboptimal decision-taking by boards.

There are three main causes of suboptimal board decisions, a toxic mixture of ignorance of board processes; the abuse of power around the boardroom table; and a willingness to avoid hard facts. As I have discussed the abuse of power in Chapter 5, let me focus here on the other two more cognitive aspects. First, ignorance of board processes. Many boards do not have an overarching, conceptual process for their collegial decision-making, nor the crucial leadership and support of the chairman to deliver the key board roles and tasks. They are often especially weak on understanding that decision-taking is a *continuing* cycle of learning from their decisions on the four board dilemmas outlined in Chapter 4, rather than a simple, binary process of saying "yes" or "no" to executives' proposals. What is usually lacking is a linked, rigorous sequence for building effective strategic decisions with imaginative ideas and authentic information through a critical review process toward the strategic decision point; and then following into implementation with rapid board learning, which, in turn, informs the next board decision-making round.

Second, the unwillingness to avoid testing hard facts. This fits with my own research findings that UK directors at least have a strong preference for relying on gut feel and soft facts ("sensing" the immediate, micro-political environment). They rely on their undoubted ability to post-rationalize their thinking and subsequent actions to satisfy themselves that they are doing their best in the best of all possible worlds. It is rare for directors to weigh the hard facts carefully before they decide what they want to believe.

As Yale psychologist Robert Sternberg has pointed out, even smart people can believe strange things. Why is this? The answer in Michael Shermer's book *Why People Believe Weird Things*[1] is that smart people are skilled at defending beliefs at which they arrived for non-smart reasons. And boards are full of smart, if not wise, people. These are a modern reinforcement of Irvin Janis's seminal groupthink studies mentioned in Chapter 5. Shermer spells out his findings thus:

Rarely do any of us sit down before a table of facts, weigh them pro and con, and choose the most logical and rational explanation, regardless of what we previously believed. Most of us, most of the time, come to our beliefs for a variety of reasons having little to do with empirical evidence and logical reasoning. Rather, such variables as genetic predisposition, parental predilection, sibling influence, peer pressure, educational experience, and life impressions, all shape the personality preferences that, in conjunction with numerous social and cultural influences, lead us to our beliefs and behaviors. We then sort through the body of data and select those that most confirm what we already believe, ignoring or rationalizing away those that do not. The phenomenon is called "confirmational bias."

As evidence he points to the US National Science Foundation's biennial report (2002) claiming, *inter alia*, that 30 percent of the US population believes in UFOs as space vehicles from other civilizations; 60 percent believes in ESP; 40 percent believes that astrology is scientific. The beliefs dropped slightly for respondents with a college education. What is especially worrying to me in terms of board and director development is Shermer's statement that 70 percent of the US population does not understand scientific process, defined in the study as comprehending probability, the experimental method, and hypothesis testing. These, plus a large dose of imagination, are the basis of effective board decision-making.

In this chapter I am suggesting a new approach to strategic thinking that I have developed with a number of boards internationally. This is based on the idea of a board's decision-making cycle being grounded firmly in my learning board model.[2] However, there is never a single, standard solution to any board's decision-making cycle. Each board will be different because of the strong, and diverse, personalities that comprise it and the combined effects of these on the final judgment. Yet I believe that there is a basic process and pattern to effective board strategic decision-making and it is this that I wish to illustrate.

Strategy and Uncertainty

Nothing is ever certain in the world of directing. Even the seemingly "easy controllables" of internal performance measures from the operational side of the business can throw up all sorts of unexpected issues when, for example, sales targets are not met, staff are unruly, budgets are overspent, project times are extended, quality is inadequate, products fail, or customers do not pay. Such examples and complaints are heard frequently around the boardroom table. However, all these examples are from the operational world of the executives. The directors are not there to resolve executive problems. They are there to oversee the pattern of executive performance and to set this within the context of delivering the board's policies and strategies. The board must not be seduced into trying to micro-manage such problems from the boardroom table.

It is the "external uncontrollables" that should be the main source of concern and focus for directors; but these are also the cause of most of their discomfort. Directors question how they can give sensible direction in an uncertain environment, yet this is what they are paid to do. Effective directors have to have a mindset that allows them to be comfortable handling high levels of uncertainty, while maintaining both their sense of direction and their moral stance. Not everyone can do that. "Control freaks" in particular make very bad directors—they cannot stand the uncertainties.

This is not a new phenomenon. Those great historic strategists Sun Tzu and Baron Carl von Clausewitz reflect across the centuries this capacity for dealing with uncertainty throughout their writings. In his classic *Vom Krieg* of 1832 Clausewitz can be paraphrased as saying:

Men cannot reduce "strategy" to a formula. Detailed planning necessarily fails, due to the inevitable frictions encountered with reality—the chance events, imperfections in execution, and the independent and the uncontrollable will of the opposition. Instead of certainty, in strategy the human elements are paramount: Leadership, morale, and the almost instinctive "feel" of the best generals are what leads to effective strategy.

It is that "feel" for the changing external environment for which effective boards strive. Under Von Moltke the Prussian general staff developed and perfected these concepts. They stressed that they did not expect any operational plan to survive beyond the first contact with the enemy; a point that still has to be drummed into all operational managers, and all directors, today. So the Prussians only drafted the broadest of objectives and strategies, and then emphasized seizing any unexpected opportunities. They stressed that strategy is not an action plan but the evolution of a key idea, I would add, through continuous learning.

The Board's Strategic Learning

All learning has a moral dimension. We learn good and bad things all of the time. The key question about board learning is whether we learn in a "good," open, questioning manner; or in a "bad," unquestioning, blame-giving, and information-hiding manner. It is crucial for directors to be viewed by their colleagues and their stakeholders as being aware of their roles, tasks, and duties, specifically in relation to the development of their strategies. To do this effectively they need to be comfortable with generating a range of discussable (not censored) ideas for implementing their strategy—and giving organizational leadership through being seen by staff and customers to learn from their decisions while living their espoused values.

It is all very well for a board to advocate the ten directoral duties discussed in Chapter 4, to sign up to them, and to go public to the shareholders and stakeholders about them. However, unless it is evident to staff, customers, stakeholders, and shareholders that the board is continuously living these espoused values through their behavior, the values are worth nothing. Indeed, they can have a negative effect on all parties involved, especially staff and customers, as disillusionment and cynicism leach energy out of the business because the directors are frequently seen not to mean what they say. If we are to avoid this, how can such noble aspirations be turned into assessable directoral behavior?

The Learning Board Process

The model that I have developed over the last 15 years to help professionalize directors is called the *learning board*. This has proved effective in bringing directors from a rudimentary understanding of their roles, tasks, and duties to becoming a more professional board. However, only if two conditions are met—that the chairman and managing director are really committed to making this happen; and that they are themselves willing to learn, and change, from joining in the board development process—can this have a chance of succeeding.

As I have written a book about the learning board—*The Fish Rots from the Head*—I will not go into the model in great detail here. What I will do is sketch quickly the main framework of the model (Figure 13) and then apply it to the board strategic decision-making cycle of learning I have developed for this book, setting the whole within the basic values of effective corporate governance: accountability, probity, and transparency to the owners.

The learning board model was constructed by beginning with the two fundamental roles of the board—driving the enterprise forward, while keeping it under prudent control—and then adding both business timespan (short term and long term) and business perspective (internal and external) dimensions. The quadrant formed is fleshed out in the first stage by adding the four key tasks of a board:

❖ Formulating policy and foresight.
❖ Strategic thinking.
❖ Supervising management,
❖ Accountability.

The context of the whole model is set within those three values of corporate governance.

Figure 13 shows the basic framework for the board. It emphasizes the classic board and directoral dilemma of having always to balance board conformance (compliance) and board performance (achievement). There is never a single "right" answer to this balancing act as the external environment is always dynamic, so it must be altered frequently; hence the need for regular and thoughtfully active board meetings. Directing is an intellectual activity above all else.

Crucial to the model is the notion of the central board role as the corporate brain striving to balance the often contradictory forces buffeting the organization. It is here that each director is expected to exercise their independent critical faculties and, to return to the ten directoral duties, their duty of critical review and independent thought, plus their duty of learning, development, appraisal, and communication.

It is this corporate brain function that connects the learning board to the wider workgroups comprising the total business. Again, as I

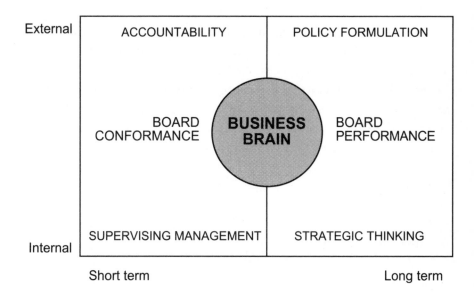

Figure 13 The learning board basic framework

have written about this extensively in *The Learning Organisation: Developing Democracy at Work* and *Twelve Organisational Capabilities: Valuing People at Work*,[3] I will simply sketch the outline of this thinking here. The argument is that any organization has three levels of learning that need to be integrated continuously through the board if the organization is to be both effective (as perceived by the external world) and efficient (as seen internally).

There are three levels of learning:

❖ *Operational*—the day-to-day, week-to-week learning that is the domain of executives and staff.
❖ *Policy*—facing up to the wider political and stakeholder issues relating to the rate of change in the organization's external environment.
❖ *Strategy*—the board and senior executives integrate the operational learning and policy learning by balancing scarce resources against the changing environment to achieve their purpose.

If the board allows policy learning to become predominant, then it can become highly intellectual but decreasingly effective as it grows detached from the reality of operational learning. If the board becomes too exercised by operational learning, a currently very common phenomenon, then over-focusing on efficiency through cost reduction, especially sacking experienced staff, leads increasingly to the well-known sequence already encountered in Chapter 6:

❖ Downsize.
❖ Rightsize.
❖ Dumbsize.
❖ Capsize.

Under this management-based approach the older, and therefore it is argued too expensive, experience base of the organization is sacked with the inevitable consequent loss of customer service, confidence, and ultimately sales. This sets off a "bad" learning circle leading to a need for even more cost reduction and so an even sharper cycle of self-induced corporate decline. While executives can convince themselves that they are right in taking such paths, it is the board's role to monitor and ensure a balance between the forces of organizational effectiveness and organizational efficiency. It should ensure that the executives give due time to the pursuit of revenue generation as well.

The four board tasks of the learning board model can be fleshed out in its time and perspective frameworks by adding detailed tasks and assessable behavior in a *cycle* of board learning (Figure 14). The sequence is as follows.

Policy formulation and foresight:

❖ Stating organizational purpose.
❖ Giving organizational vision and values.
❖ Creating an effective emotional climate and organizational culture.
❖ Monitoring the external environment.

The first three above are the energy sources of the whole organization—the "heart of the business."

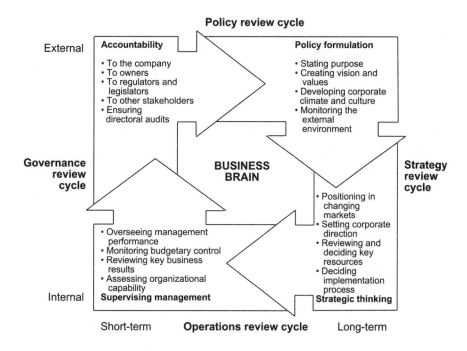

Figure 14 The learning board model

The link to *strategic thinking* is through the board's crucial strategic debates and risk assessments on the relationship between "monitoring the external environment" and "positioning in changing markets." This is *the* crucial debate of the board. These decisions are the future lifeblood of the organization because they generate the future revenue streams and lead to:

❖ Setting corporate direction.
❖ Reviewing and deciding key resources.
❖ Deciding implementation processes.

The second crucial board debate is over the relationship between "implementing strategy" and "ensuring organizational capabilities," which test whether the proposed strategy is workable and properly resourced. The consequent board and executive learning from this helps inform the rest of the *supervising management* tasks:

❖ Reviewing key business results.
❖ Monitoring budgetary control.
❖ Overseeing management performance.

Ultimately, *accountability* returns to take the prime place in the board's annual learning cycle, as the board alone is responsible for the total control and performance of the business and by ensuring honest directoral audits, must account for its stewardship in order of legal precedence to:

❖ The company (as a separate legal personality).
❖ The owners.
❖ The regulators and legislators.
❖ The other stakeholders.

These elements are not simply boxes for ticking by the board to show that its members fulfill everything required legally of them. They are key elements of a dynamic corporate/social network and a series of learning processes that interact and change continuously to give an overall assessment of the state of the business.

As board tasks are essentially process driven, there is a natural *rhythm* for any board that is derived from the learning board model. This is why it is drawn with arrows driving into and out of each quarter. The basic board rhythm is annual for completion of the total cycle, but areas such as strategic thinking must have significant board time dedicated to them at least quarterly, and the supervising management aspect needs at least a monthly brief, critical review. Time budgeting of the annual board cycle by the chairman and company secretary is crucial if the directors are to be able to be appraised as effective. Without this the board is liable to slip back into the abuse of power by strong personalities taking over, and subsequent decision-taking being by post-rationalization of their wishes. All directors should have every board meeting in their diary a year ahead, know the position of each meeting on the board's learning cycle, and be fully prepared.

Developing Effective Board Strategic Decision-Taking

At the center of the natural cycle that a learning board needs to follow to fulfill its responsibilities is another crucially important process—the strategic decision-taking cycle. This is the board's energy source. It uses the framework of the learning board cycle but goes into much greater detail. By so doing the effectiveness and optimization of the board's information-gathering, idea-generating, risk-assessment, values-testing, and decision-taking processes are exposed to full critical review and debate by the board. From this analysis the board learns about its effectiveness in the eyes of its shareholders and stakeholders through testing against the reality of its espoused strategies.

The strategic decision-taking cycle is a way of countering my research finding of the pernicious effects of directors' tendencies to rely too much on gut feel, sensing, and the over-use of soft facts in their thinking styles. The cycle helps adds rigor to what can otherwise be a very one-sided, executive-dominated process. Most importantly, it encourages a board to comply with both the Turnbull Report and the Myners' Report in their push for board performance and director competence.

The Strategic Decision-Taking Cycle

Before going into any detail on the board's decision-taking cycle, it is essential that any board budgets time with its senior executives to determine who will do what in terms of policy and strategy. It needs to agree a strategy development and implementation process (Figure 15). Many problems in developing and implementing strategy arise simply because there is little clarity between the board and its executives about this. Each party needs certainty as to which responsibilities, decisions, and processes are strictly the board's, which are the executives', and which need joint agreement and monitoring. This may seem so blindingly obvious as to be banal, but in practice great uncertainty is often generated because of confusion as to who has which authority.

Stage of strategy development	Board authorities	Managerial authorities	Clarifying joint or unclearly assigned authorities
Developing strategy	• Understand the external environment/changes • Main forum for debate and discussion of vision, values, goals, and key issues • Develop and agree vision, values, and culture • Provide advice and support to executives during the development of the plan • Comment on executives' drafts • Check compliance accountabilities • Agree final structure of strategy	• Undertake research to provide information for the development of the strategy • Embed the learning organization culture throughout the organization • Provide feedback on environmental scanning rapidly to the board	• Who will write drafts of strategy and implementation plans • Who will agree the use of consultants and advisers • Who will control the budget for strategy development
Ratifying the strategy	• Approve strategy implementation and feedback process • Delegate to senior management/executives	• Present implementation plan to board • Develop implementation plan • Allocate resources to implementation	• Who will disseminate the strategy • Who will complete the details of the strategy
Monitoring implementation	• Monitor overall progress of strategy implementation • Help executives in problem-solving and troubleshooting • Communicating with shareholders/stakeholders	• Manage implementation process • Measure progress • Manage resource committed • Sign off complete tasks • Report frequently to the board	• Who is responsible for speed and frequency of feedback
Developing partnerships and alliances	• Identify and approach potential partners • Use board networks • Communicate with existing partners • Approve formal partnerships and alliances	• Help identify potential partners • Help approach potential partners • Negotiate detailed agreements • Manage partnerships and alliances	• Who will finalize partnership agreements

Figure 15 Strategy development and implementation process

Figure 15 illustrates in a simple framework the type of authorities that need to be agreed by directors and executives before the whole strategic decision-taking exercise is launched. It can be seen as a development of the document on the reserved powers of the board. Both are hugely valuable in focusing scarce directoral and executive energies, and both are usually under-valued.

The board's strategic decision-taking cycle (Figure 16) breaks into six distinct but strongly interactive phases:

❖ Information codification and due diligence.
❖ Idea generation.
❖ Risk assessment.
❖ Values checking.
❖ Decision-taking.
❖ Implementation and learning.

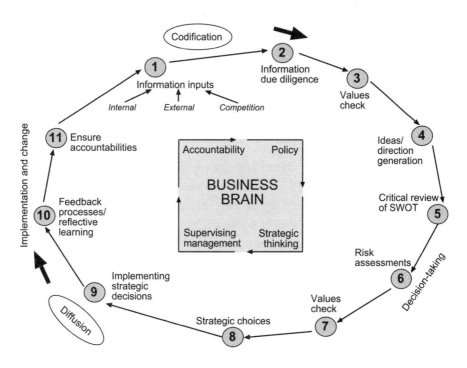

Figure 16 Strategic decision-taking cycle

The total board strategic decision-taking cycle has 11 sequential and closely related elements to it:

1 Information inputs.
2 Information due diligence.
3 Values check of due diligence.
4 Idea generation and critique.
5 Comparison with SWOT analysis.
6 Risk assessments.
7 Values check of risk assessments.
8 Strategic choices.
9 Implementing strategic decisions.
10 Feedback and board learning.
11 Checking accountabilities.

A detailed analysis of each of these elements defines much of a real board's effective working time. The 11 elements need to be learned and relearned by the board so that it can fulfill its functions of the duties of care, independent thought and criticism, and learning.

1 Information Inputs

Data is not information. Data is that sea of facts with which we all feel continually overwhelmed. The directoral art lies in using discerning questions, backed by intelligent naïveté, to tease from the data the specific information needed to solve the problem at hand.

   Such information comes from three main sources.

External world information
This involves sifting the ever-changing data from changes in the:

❖ Political and legislative environment.
❖ Physical environment.
❖ Economic environment.
❖ Social environment.

- ❖ Technological environment.
- ❖ Trade environment.

This PPESTT analysis takes a little learning before it is used as an automatic tool within a board to help derive its crucial forward-looking areas of policy formulation and foresight. To encourage the development of each director's helicopter view, I often use a "buddy system" over an 18-month period so that each director spends three months monitoring each of the six PPESTT aspects, working with a peer or senior executive on a mini research project, so that they become comfortable asking questions on each aspect. This deliberately takes single-function directors way beyond their previous mindsets. In this way two objectives are achieved. First, within 18 months the board becomes much more highly sensitized to changes in the external environment. Second, its members are more comfortable, individually and collectively, working with these "uncontrollable" areas and asking discerning questions about them.

Comparative world information

A key part of this information-gathering process involves monitoring the absolute and relative performance of your company against known customers and competitors. While there is growing awareness of the need for continuing customer information, such systematic competitor analysis is still fairly rare, except in the retail trade. Indeed, many think it not quite right to "spy" on competitors. I am not talking about spying. I mean the regular and systematic gathering of competitor data from which good-quality information can be cheaply derived.

We all like to boast, and chairmen and managing directors are particularly prone to this. Boasting is part of "competitive greed." Cost-effective competitor analysis is different. A careful reading of annual reports, company statements, press releases, and competitors' websites can prove highly enlightening. So can hanging around conferences, trade fairs, and industry events—provided that you know what you are looking and listening for. You need to have in mind such questions as:

❖ What are our customers saying about us?

❖ How well are our competitors doing?

❖ Which changes are they discussing?

❖ How is the sector doing overall?

❖ What are the new issues arising for the sector?

❖ Are we using appropriate benchmarks to measure our comparative performance?

❖ What is happening in non-industry-related areas that may have an impact on us later?

Above all, we must ask: "How do we *know* this—how accurate are our sources of information?"

Internal world information

My approach to processing internally generated information was spelt out in detail in Chapter 6. I will repeat here that the board's job is to oversee the pattern of executive outputs using the directoral dashboard, not to try to micro-manage the operations of the business from the boardroom. This takes some learning, under the leadership of a competent chairman.

The detailed feedback coming from the learning board processes, especially the supervising management and accountabilities quarters, gives hard information on actual business performance. This can be difficult to access and discuss on some boards because of their preference for using soft facts (assumptions, hunches, and guesses) and being more comfortable with gut-feel data and pre-judged values, while downgrading the importance of hard facts, rationality, and ingenuity.

At this point such integrative tools as the balanced scorecard,[4] the European Business Excellence Model,[5] and the service/profit chain[6] come into their own. They not only give readings on the performance of specific functions within the business, but also allow directors to begin to take a helicopter view and see the relationship of each specialist function to the others. Over time the board can track the trends and so monitor if things are getting out of balance.

Questions can be asked such as:

- ❖ Where are we adding shareholder value?
- ❖ How is the market changing?
- ❖ What are the customer satisfaction/churn rates?
- ❖ Are there functions that are getting out of line in budgetary terms?
- ❖ Where are we likely to have to rebalance our strategic allocation of scarce resources?
- ❖ What do our financial ratios and trend lines tell us?
- ❖ What do our human resources ratios and trend lines tell us?
- ❖ Are there any internal audit issues of which we should be aware?
- ❖ Are there any external audit issues of which we should be aware?

Such questioning would be handled as a natural part of an effective board's monthly routine until members are used to the rhythm and trust the answers. This part of the strategic decision-taking process should not take more than an hour at a each board meeting, once the system is up and running. If it does, this is usually a sign that the board is trying to micro-manage the executives from the boardroom and is not getting on with its professional job of directing.

2 Information Due Diligence

Many boards are not rigorous in their codification of information. It is very tempting merely to allow the board's power players to have their say, demand that their information is used without question, and, provided that it sounds reasonable, for the other directors simply to say "yes." Remember that from my research most directors are very comfortable with their gut feel and sensing thinking styles, and are skillful at post-rationalizing these without careful consideration of the hard facts. If you add the bullying and "shaping" characteristics of power players on the other board members, it is easy to understand (but not to forgive) that, while some directors may not be committed to the decision, many just feel that in the short term acquiescence is more comfortable. As shareholders become more litigious this tendency to avoid the duties of care, critical review, independent thought, and learning is increasingly threatening to a director's personal and family wealth and personal esteem, as well as to their future corporate career.

So what can be done by the average, not very courageous director to ensure that these directoral duties are carried out? Businesses with well-developed business intelligence units tend to scan all data with a cynical eye before they accept it as valid. Their way of testing what is being used as information to solve a problem is always to ask four fundamental questions:

- ❖ What is the source of this data?
- ❖ Is this source reliable?
- ❖ How do we know that this data is valid?
- ❖ How can we cross-check this data?

This may sound as dry as dust but, remembering that many directors will only be used to processing soft data, it is crucial that they do critically question each other's information base. This does not invalidate the collection of soft data by hanging around chatting at conferences while listening to gossip, idle or otherwise; but such data does need to be treated with discretion. Ensuring the validity of the information on which key strategic decisions will be based is a key part of the director's role, reinforced by the chairman as a neutral facilitator.

Information security

If many boards are lax in their information-codification processes, they are even weaker in ensuring the security of the information collected. We all know about teenage hackers penetrating US security systems, banks allowing personal data to be displayed thoughtlessly on e-banking systems, and the mindless generation of too obvious security codes allowing access to confidential corporate, and personal, information. The issue of a company's and board's information security could be a book in itself. Rather than attempt that here, I shall signal the crucial importance of the issue and refer the reader to the Information Security Forum,[7] whose long-term research is worth careful study and adoption, especially as they are beginning to link effective corporate governance with information-based risk assessment.

3 Values Check of Due Diligence

Before rushing to the strategic decision process itself, it is wise for the board to pause and consider whether the way in which the information is being gathered and processed is legally and ethically acceptable, and secure, within the three values of corporate governance. Has it been collected in a manner for which the directors can comfortably be held legally accountable, or does it break criminal or civil laws, for example intellectual property laws? Has the information been collected in an honest manner? And is the information-collection process capable of being explained openly to the owners and the courts?

Do reputation and probity really matter?

Many directors ridicule such questioning of information-collecting values and rely on their illusions of invulnerability and moral superiority to get them by, hoping that they will not be found out or scrutinized. However, these values questions are precisely those that may need to be defended in a court and now fall firmly within the legal area of "discoverability." If handled crassly, this is where the company's reputation can be damaged badly.

Does this matter? Yes, a great deal. The US Federal Reserve estimated in 2002 that 50 years ago the intangible assets of a company—intellectual property rights, business reputation, and brand equity—accounted for around 22 percent of the average listed company's net worth. Now the Fed estimates that they make up 47 percent of net worth and rising. The percentage is higher in service industries and especially in finance and banking, where customers demand certainty. This includes absolute probity in the collection and handling of data on which strategic judgments are then made.

When Hill & Knowlton did a survey of US corporations in 2002 it found that reputation management is considered so important that 38 percent treat it as a board-level function; 35 percent had the CEO's compensation linked directly to "protecting and enhancing the company's reputation"; 46 percent of the respondents linked company reputation directly to the personality of the man or woman in the CEO seat. And 88 percent of the senior executives surveyed said that in future the management of the company's reputation will be a major factor in the choice of board directors and top executives.

If the board's information-collection process is handled professionally, this values check sets a healthy governance framework with which to start the next part of the strategic decision-taking process: the idea-generation comparisons and risk-assessment processes. If not, the mis-collection of information can seriously damage a corporation's health.

4 Idea Generation and Critique

This is the point on the learning board model where the board's "monitoring of the external environment" processes meets its fundamental "positioning in changing markets" debate. It is the crucial debate for any board. This is the source of business strategy.

Nevertheless, idea generation is often treated superficially by board members because of two blockages within them. First, their discomfort with budgeting time to debate the "intellectual" issues of what is occurring in the outside world and how they position their scarce resources in relation to that—their business strategy. Second, the abuse of power by one or two dominant individuals on the board to achieve their own ends regardless of the company's strategic interests.

Complexity and board thinking processes

Because many boards are habituated simply to discussing one idea and then being led rapidly to an "obvious" conclusion by a chairman with a convergent thinking style, they often question me about why I bother with this part of the decision-making process at all. My answer is that it reduces their personal liability by demonstrating the best use of the existing diversity of experiences around the boardroom table to generate higher-quality debate and critical review.

These lead to optimal decisions that, in turn, add value for the owners. In contrast, many directors see all life as binary—there is only ever one answer, and if that doesn't work then you keep on trying until you find a question that fits your answer.

I take the trouble for two further, more detailed reasons. First, because over-rapid convergent decision-making usually leads to sub-optimal decisions. You cannot get a quality, tested decision if you only have one idea to work on. President Kennedy found this out in the time between his binary thinking approach that led to the Bay of Pigs disaster and, only nine months later, the "open critical review with no personal comeback" approach that led to the successful outcome of the Cuban missile crisis.

The second reason is that life is complex and uncertain. Chance can be cause. This complexity therefore requires that an attitude be taken to board decision-making that accepts and uses such uncertainty. A board needs a "both… and" approach to its thinking, rather than "either… or." That is when things can get tough. Many directors with whom I work have an anti-intellectual approach to their decision-making, demonstrating the naïve belief that an early total commitment to a single idea and plan will see them through the roughest water. Therefore, they argue, little time should be spent exploring alternatives, building contingency plans, and ensuring rapid feedback processes to test the implementation of their strategy. However, the skills of handling and *using* uncertainty and ambiguity are crucial to optimal board decision-taking and learning.

What can be done to open up a board's thinking so that it becomes comfortable with a process that begins with *divergent thinking* and the open exploration of alternatives, continues with contingency plans, and finally returns to the over-comfortable ground of *convergent thinking* and judgment prior to committing to a board decision?

The first step is to ensure that the board has time and space to think. In the learning board model the minimum necessary is the agreed systematic use of at least a quarterly strategic thinking away-day for the board, with no other agenda items, to ensure that there is at least the space to do the necessary critical thinking and consequent decision-taking. Such strategic thinking awaydays need be put in all board members' diaries at least a year ahead and the chairman must make it clear that it is a sackable offense for any director not to attend.

However, then awful reality cuts in. A board away from base, with the phones switched off and only strategic thinking on the agenda, can feel like a lonely place—unless you have quality ideas and information to debate. Breaking out of convergent thinking styles can often require a homeopathic dose of external facilitation. The biggest issue is often not the lack of intellectual capability on the board, but rather the mind-guarding and self-censoring that block their generation of ideas and information in the first place. An external view can help free that logjam.

What can be done to ease such mind-guarding and self-censorship? Much depends on the quality of chairmanship. As discussed in Chapter 3, the chairman is charged with optimizing the quality of the decision-taking process and maintaining the corporate governance values of the board. So he must ensure that he maintains a neutral role on all matters under discussion to seek out the highest-quality information available, and to record where no valid ideas or information are to be found. As most chairmen are not trained to do this, it does not usually get done.

How can this blockage be opened up? There are a number of well-known techniques for ensuring that at the start ideas are put before the group without censorship or immediate evaluation by any member. Three processes that have stood the test of time are Tony Buzan's mind maps,[8] Edward De Bono's six thinking hats,[9] and Jerry Rhodes' Thinking Intentions Profile.[10] The use of any of these three instruments is advocated to release the creation of better-quality ideas and so better inform the board's risk-assessment and decision-making processes.

Mind maps

The most easily used of these is the mind map or radiant thinking process developed by Tony Buzan. The crux of this is to get board members to generate lots of ideas and then, very importantly, to record them *without* critical comment or assessment, by generating on a flipchart a mind map radiating in all directions from the central statement of the issue under discussed. The resulting "spidergram" (it usually looks like a spider's web of ideas) can later be dissected, debated, and then evaluated. Finally, possible solutions and risks are prioritized, tested, and selected.

The beauty of mind maps is that you can get everything on to one flipchart or screen and everyone can participate without the censorship of immediate evaluation. The resulting quality of ideas and information input immediately raises the likelihood of optimizing decision-taking. It also leaves a record of ideas that have been rejected but might need to be reconsidered during the contingency planning process.

Six thinking hats

De Bono's "six thinking hats" approach builds on the notion of there being six definable thinking styles at work in a group and that understanding your personal balance allows you, and other board members, to play to your strengths. This enhances the board's decision-taking competence by helping each member to "gate keep" the board's positive and negative thinking dynamics.

The six hats are:

- ❖ *White hat*—neutral and objective, focuses on facts and figures.
- ❖ *Red hat*—focuses on people's feelings, emotions, and responses.
- ❖ *Yellow hat*—focuses on being positive and constructive, sees the benefits in each idea.
- ❖ *Black hat*—focuses on giving critical assessment (but not negativity).
- ❖ *Green hat*—focuses on creativity, provides new angles to ideas.
- ❖ *Blue hat*—focuses on being the "chair," controls the flow of the group and ensures that all hats are used during the problem-solving process.

It takes only a little time working with a board to demonstrate that if each of them is constrained by using only one over-dominant thinking hat, frustration builds very quickly. This is particularly true if someone whose preference is black hat is asked to wear a white or blue hat. The subsequent learning about how this particular board works, and what can be done to open up the channels of thinking prior to evaluation and decision-taking, can be deep.

TIPs and THUNKS

I frequently use the Thinking Intentions Profile (TIP) inventory and its deeper analytical sister THUNKS to help a board understand seriously its need to both widen and deepen its thinking portfolio.

The six basic TIP categories are:

- ❖ *Judgment* (past oriented), divided into two subsets of:
  —Logic/rationality.
  —Values.
- ❖ *Describe* (present oriented), divided into two subsets of:
  —Hard facts.
  —Soft facts.
- ❖ *Realize* (future oriented), divided into two subsets of:
  —Ingenuity.
  —Vision.

An initial rough-cut of the TIP gives individual board members their primary scores, which can then be aggregated to show the pattern of thinking preferences for the board as a working group. This information is usually sufficient for the issue of board thinking preferences to be taken seriously, particularly if the prevalent pattern of habitually preferring soft facts, logic, and vision is clearly seen to over-ride the use of hard facts and ingenuity. From this personal data it is possible to go into much more sophisticated analysis of 21 elements of individual thinking preferences—the "THUNKS"—that leads to both individual and board development plans.

5 Comparison with SWOT Analysis

Despite all the rhetoric in business schools about the use of increasingly complex analytical strategic tools, the reality around the board-room table is that in the end strategic decisions are often taken on one

	Internal	External
To protect and develop	STRENGTHS	OPPORTUNITIES
To reduce and avoid	WEAKNESSES	THREATS

Figure 17 SWOT analysis

or two simple propositions, presented on one piece of paper. Indeed, I argue that they must be to preserve the board's sanity. As the future of the business hangs on such decisions, it is crucial that these propositions are clear and well informed. My colleagues and I have written extensively about the range of tools for strategic analysis and decision-making in *Developing Strategic Thought*,[11] so I will not repeat the detail here.

Despite being accused by colleagues of being wildly old-fashioned, I start with the use of a one-page SWOT analysis (reviewing Strengths and Weaknesses, Opportunities and Threats) as the board's initial and final focus before their eventual decision-making.

As the SWOT is such a well-known tool I will not describe it here. However, from years of working with boards I have learned to stress two points about it (Figure 17). First, the key focus of the strengths and weaknesses side of the quadrant is internal to the organization; and the opportunities and threats are essentially based on an analysis of the changing external world. There are many tools around to flesh out the details. For example, as shown in Chapter 6, to generate the internal, strengths and weaknesses, perspective I could start with a value chain analysis[12] to test and develop the validity of the board's assumptions. To generate information and debate about the external, opportunities and threats, perspective I could use a five forces analysis[13] to help start and develop the often difficult board debate about how the future will evolve—the foresight aspects of the learning board model.

Second, as a key part of information due diligence, it is crucial to measure the board's understanding of each quadrant of the SWOT against known competitors. While this may seem blindingly obvious, it is remarkable how many SWOTs are developed without reference to competitor positioning. A great deal of information about future plans can be found in the trade press, analysts' reports, on the competitor's website, in chairmen's statements (they do have an ego and like to boast about "their" company), and at public conferences. The trick is to be aware of, and sensitive to, what you are seeking as information about your competitors to better inform your own board's SWOT.

6 Risk Assessments

It is only at this point in the board's decision-taking cycle that its critical review and independent thought processes are fully brought into play. It is also here that mind-guarding and self-censorship are the most tempting option for many executive directors. So it is important for the chairman to ensure that there is plenty of time to debate the many and varied risks that any proposed strategy will necessarily create.

What are these risks? The word "risk" entered the English language from the old Italian *riscare*, meaning "to dare." Risk-taking is the essence of capitalism—daring to put capital at risk to add value—and by the fifteenth century was well developed in Italian city states such as Venice and Genoa. It concerns the real, or possible, events that reduce the likelihood of reaching business goals, and increase the probability of losses. At board level risk is, therefore, concerned with assessing the probability, and the consequences, of such events affecting the desired outcomes, and of reducing the uncertainties in turbulent and dynamic internal and external environments. Risk assessment is never an exact science, as it relies on the judgment of the directors.

The Turnbull Report[14] asks the following of UK directors:

When reviewing reports annually the board should:

❖ *Consider what are the significant risks and assess how they have been identified, evaluated and managed.*
❖ *Assess the effectiveness of the related internal control systems for significant risks, noting any significant failings or weaknesses reported.*
❖ *Consider whether the findings indicate a need for more extensive monitoring of the internal control system.*

It also states:

The Board's annual assessment should consider:
❖ *Changes since the last review in the nature and extent of significant risks and the company's ability to respond effectively to changes in its business and external environment.*
❖ *The scope and quality of management's monitoring of risks and systems of internal control, and the work of the internal audit function and other providers of assurance.*
❖ *The extent and the frequency of the communication of results of such monitoring of the board, or board committees, to build its cumulative assessment of internal control and risk management.*
❖ *The incident of significant control failings or weaknesses identified ... and the extent that they have resulted in unforeseen outcomes ... that may have an impact on future company performances.*
❖ *The effectiveness of the company's public reporting process.*

What are the risks that need to be assessed? A typical list for rigorous and regular board review would cover:

❖ Reputation risk.
❖ Financial risk.
❖ Political risk.

❖ Country risk.
❖ Terrorism risk.
❖ Legislative risk.
❖ Regulatory risk.
❖ Health and safety risk.
❖ Physical environmental risk.
❖ Human rights risk.
❖ Information security risk.
❖ Supply chain risk.
❖ Intellectual property risk.

Some risk assessment can be handled mathematically using actuarial processes, probability theory, and gaming theory. However, not all risks are easily susceptible to such quantification and so there is a need to rely on the subjective judgment of the directors working as a board and their continuing sensitivity to changes in the external environment. Here the board is "learning in the headlights" as it tries to resolve the traditional directoral dilemma of how to drive the enter-

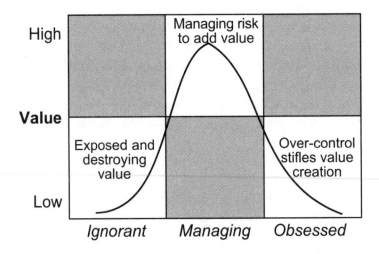

Figure 18 Risk appetite

Source: KPMG, reproduced by permission.

prise forward while keeping it under prudent control. There is no easy answer, but such decisions will have to be defended in public more frequently in the future.

The list above may seem intimidatingly long, but only a handful of these risks will need active consideration at any one time by any well-organized board. The rest will be reported on regularly and frequently through a trusted internal audit function.

I cannot over-emphasize the importance of internal audit in identifying and handling complex business risks. The internal auditors can very quickly identify matters going off track or failing compliance. The trick is for them to have a direct line, instant access, to the managing director and chairman outside the normal line-reporting structure. They must not be blocked by more senior mind guards. They are crucial "whistleblowers" who need to be listened to by the chairman and the board, especially the audit committee, regardless of any director's, or senior executive's, personal power.

If a board remains in blissful ignorance of the risks to which it is exposing the company, then its members are in dereliction of their directoral duty. If they are intimidated into inaction by being over-fixated on risk assessments, they are equally liable. There is no getting away from the fact that directing is about the exercise of judgment by the board on behalf of the owners.

7 Values Check of Risk Assessments

Before going into the final lap of the strategic decision-taking process, it is wise for a board to pause and check that it is complying with its two sets of values. The first check is that the three values of corporate governance—accountability, probity, and transparency—are operating effectively on behalf of the owners.

The second is that the espoused corporate values underwritten by the board are also incorporated into the proposition being debated. Corporate values statements are notoriously difficult for a board to be seen to live by. It is very easy for directors' words to be out of sync with their behavior; and staff and customers tend only to believe the behavior.

As an example, I was working on strategy and change with the board of a major bank. At the same time the company was running a "Values Statement Project." The board members had a great time determining a list of corporate values that they then intended to publish to staff and customers. To their annoyance I asked if they had tested the values on a sample of staff and customers. I stressed that it would be impossible for staff to commit to something to which they had given no input; and that potentially raising unrealistic expectations in their customers was likely to damage the brand severely.

After some grumbling they decided to do the testing. One of the values was "honesty"—a key value for any bank. To the board's horror they had a 100 percent response from both staff and customers that it was not an honest bank. It was not that it was venal—if you put your money in it did stay there—but rather that over many decades the bank had developed an internal culture of "never give a customer a fair chance." It did not tell existing customers of better deals, it held on to transfer monies a day or two longer than other banks, making more on interest for itself, and so on.

There is now a board debate on whether honesty should be a key value for the bank. The answer looks as though it must be "yes" (did any director really doubt this?), but the board is very aware that to be seen to live this value it will have to change both operating procedures and the internal organizational culture in a significant and painful way, with the risk of upsetting shareholders at least in the short term until staff are committed to the espoused values and customers believe them.

8 Strategic Choices

The preceding seven decision-taking steps end with a focus on the board's strategic choices. This is the point in the learning board model where the "monitoring the external environment" and "positioning in changing markets" debates are brought to a conclusion. The answer is usually more subtle than a mere "yes."

Many directors are surprised to find that there are only five strategic decisions to be taken and that the "answer" is usually a subtle blend of all of them. The strategic decisions are:

❖ Advance.
❖ Retreat.
❖ Hold our ground.
❖ Make alliances.
❖ Withdraw.

It is the combination of these choices, and the subsequent effectiveness of their implementation, that ultimately determine the board's competence. This is where the directors place their bets, while striving not to bet the whole company's future on one throw of the dice. This is where board performance is determined.

Because many books have been written on strategic decision-taking—see for example Gerry Johnson's writing,[15] Max Boisot's fascinating C-Space work,[16] and books by Gary Hamel[17]—I will merely mention two aspects of the current debate. First, the decision to "hold our ground" is not a "free" option. In a turbulent world scarce resources must be used to hold that position, which will leave fewer for *advancing* into new markets or new products and services; or for *making alliances* with new players or existing competitors—the notion of co-opetition[18] where you have to both compete and cooperate with the same player simultaneously.

Secondly, an often forgotten aspect of strategic decision-taking is the board's duty to draw up contingency plans. Strategies rarely roll out smoothly, and operational plans never do. As soon as executives meet the reality of the marketplace they have to adjust their plans thoughtfully and rapidly. If these adjustments are significant, then there is a need for very fast feedback to the board on the robustness, or otherwise, of its strategy. Directors need the humility to learn fast and to adjust their strategy, or abandon it, quickly.

The key to board performance is to record these decisions and then rigorously return to them, at least each quarter, to review them critically.

9 Implementing Strategic Decisions

A half-decent strategy well implemented by the board and its executives is worth much more to a business than a brilliant strategy that cannot be properly implemented. So a board needs to have an early measure of whether it has the organizational capability to deliver its strategy. Since I have written previously about such measurements,[19] I shall only mention here the necessary conditions for the effective implementation of any strategy.

Board members must ensure that the following are true:

* Their organizational purpose is clear and communicated.
* Their organizational vision is understood and accepted.
* Their organizational values are understood, accepted, and built into the appraisal system.
* Their strategic decisions are clear and communicated.
* Their words are seen to be in line with their espoused values and behavior in pursuing the strategy.
* Their business, funding, and people strategies are clear and communicated.
* Project management systems are in place to give rapid and continuous feedback on the implementation of the strategy.
* The board has created the emotional climate in the company to allow open learning and critical review among its executives, staff, and customers.

These are heroic assumptions for many companies. It is essential that they are tested before the rollout of the strategy. Differential measures of where the company is now, and where it needs to be to achieve its goals, are needed on each of the 12 organizational capabilities:

* Adaptability.
* Work quality.
* Clarity of personal responsibility.
* Financial rewards.
* Personal rewards.

- ❖ Organizational clarity.
- ❖ Personal performance measures.
- ❖ Group performance measures.
- ❖ Learning climate.
- ❖ Leadership.
- ❖ Customer orientation.
- ❖ Competitor orientation.

Differential measures are necessary but alone are not sufficient for implementation. They need to be put into a framework that the board can see and monitor over time as the changes are rolled out. Figure 19 shows this relationship model.

Figure 19 Organizational capability survey

The problem for both the board and executives is that the model clearly shows the paradox that while they can control the top half, it is the bottom two sectors that determine the staff's energy and commitment that will be put into the implementation process. And that is controlled directly only by the individuals themselves and the small workgroups that are their day-to-day working life. No matter how hard the bosses shout, the work flow and quality are ultimately determined by whether people actually want to work with you.

So how do you motivate people in times of great uncertainty and change?

10 Feedback and Board Learning

We know that any change announced will send the vast majority of executives and staff into a natural, but depressive, downward spiral, as shown in Figure 20.

The question is what the board can do to ensure that this downward spiral is as short as possible. Whether the issue is a major organizational change required from existing staff to implement the new strategy or the acquisition and merger of two very different organizations, I suggest two specific activities that the board needs to ensure that the executives undertake. First, before any changes are announced the executives are tasked to ensure that a "stability group," or groups, is set up to keep the basic organizational wheels turning even at the height of company's destabilization. This may mean doing deals with trade unions and other interest groups. Fine—you need to ensure that these people feel stable enough in their contractual relationship and know that for the next n months or years they will be protected.

Second, ideally before the change or very soon after it, action-learning groups should be established to pilot, or publicly model, the nature of the key changes expected if the strategy is to be delivered. These changes can easily be identified through the differential measures from an organizational capability survey. It is imperative that the board ensures that these results are widely published and discussed within the organization.

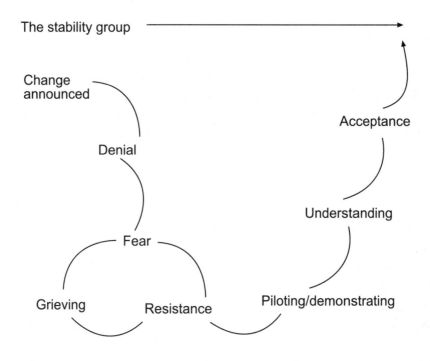

Figure 20 Unblocking resistance to change

Then volunteers are called for to work, full- or part-time, on each of the key issues identified in an open action-learning process. These volunteers should comprise a group of six to eight people mixed diagonally across the organization structure from senior to very junior, but all committed to working collegially. They will add their diverse experiences to their problem analysis and, very importantly, will be able to tap information and energy sources from their own parts of the organization. They will help with regularly encouraging all members of the organization to debate both with the action-learning groups and through open, monthly feedback meetings of the whole company on their progress. This leads to remarkably fast and effective organizational change in pursuit of a strategy to which they have contributed, and will continue to add, their feedback, ideas, action, and therefore their commitment. It is the speed and honesty of this feedback that determine the effectiveness of the strategy implementation.

11 Checking Accountabilities

The board's decision-taking round is completed by a final accountabilities check, usually around month nine of the financial year so that
there is time to rectify any issues before the regulators take an interest. Using the learning board model, the board can ensure that it is in
compliance with the law and agreements with all the stakeholder
groups.

These stakeholders will include:

❖ The company as a legal personality in its own right.
❖ The owners.
❖ Legislators.
❖ Regulators.
❖ Customers.
❖ Staff.
❖ Suppliers.
❖ Representatives of local communities.
❖ Representatives of the physical environment.

These stakeholders create a complex web of relationships to which
the board is ultimately accountable. Some boards do not like this; a
few resent it bitterly. Nevertheless, there is increasingly little they can
do about it since, as we have seen throughout this book, there is a
global move to reinforce both the law and the regulatory context and
mechanisms that govern boards. Corporate governance has come to
stay.

Blockages to Developing the Learning Board

Over the past five years I have developed many boards to their satisfaction, but my own major learning has been through three failures of
board development. While this is a tiny percentage of my total work,
these failures are very instructive. I have had three separate managing
directors stop the board development process abruptly when they

found that it discomforted them and when the chairman was not willing to face the issues that it was creating.

As an example, in one case what stopped the board development process was not the insight that the managing directors had from their peers and direct reports on their own behavior, or even on their only partial understanding of the directoral roles and tasks. Rather, what threw them was the worrying amount of high-quality, new information released suddenly in their decision-taking processes through the added rigor of a systematic board development process. Information that had been held back by directors and senior executives through self-censorship, untested assumptions, bullying, and mind-guarding was suddenly available. The immediate results were very uncomfortable all round. The board development process was stopped abruptly and the MD insisted that they progressed using the wrong information.

In another instance the board, working for the first time as a collegial group, showed the managing director that his business plan for the next three years was fundamentally flawed, since the figures that had been agreed only recently could not be justified. The directors had either self-censored the data or had not fought to debate the hard facts for fear of upsetting the MD. He had been keen to rush the business planning process through to achieve the figures that he felt he needed for his own rewards. He was furious that this new information came out, because he had submitted the business plan to group head office under the impression that all the board agreed with his figures. The MD had made the fatal assumption that silence meant assent. He had not tested his own board's commitment to the business plan, nor had the chairman.

Yet rather than treat the new information as true and deal with it quickly, the MD chose to attack his own board for a lack of loyalty to him—a classic bullying tactic. They were shocked and horrified and retreated into taciturnity, having no doubt of the MD's obvious lack of commitment to them and to the very board development process that he had so recently initiated. However, two other issues remained in the minds of those board members. First, there was a bitter taste left by the MD saying that he was keen on the board development process, getting his peers energized by it, and then leaving them in the lurch as soon as things got tough. Second, they now had new knowledge and aspirations on how they wanted the board to be run in the future and to what end, and so started a plan to rid themselves of the MD. Needless to say, the chairman was a weak and nominal figure who delegated all board power to the MD and failed completely to fill his "boss of the board" role. The MD learned the very hard lesson that board development is much more than merely a training program.

A Continuous Cycle of Board Learning

The end of a board's decision-taking cycle is not the end of its learning. It is simply the start of a new round of higher-quality learning. The quality and quantity of their learning need to be fed back into the information inputs to trigger a new cycle. Hopefully the sum of that learning will take the board's decision-taking cycle up a pitch so that the quality of learning during the next cycle will be much improved. It is to professionalizing the board that we turn in the next chapter.

CHAPTER EIGHT

Professionalizing the Board

Appraisal, Training, and Accreditation

D IRECTING WILL BECOME A RECOGNIZED PROFESSION internationally over the next two decades. The pressures for improving board performance mentioned in Chapter 2 are growing too strongly for them to be stopped. What is now obsolescent, and will soon be obsolete, is the all-too-common notion that a few amateur friends of the chief executive and chairman can enjoy some good food and wine, lots of golf, and somehow fit in a bit of time to give guidance to the company and add value for the owners in the long term.

Figure 21 shows the four main board types. This book argues that what is needed is the *professional board*.

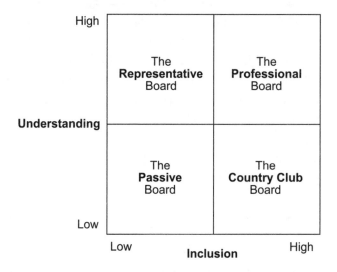

Figure 21 **The emotional climate of boards**

What, then, comprises board and directoral sufficiency? Before we go into any detail, remember that Chapter 6 stressed that such processes and competences must be measurable, otherwise they will not be seen by either the directors or the owners as valid. This means that all boards need a regular, rigorous, and quantifiable *appraisal* system. The system must measure both the effectiveness of the whole board as a working group and of each director as an individual member of the board. It must do this with both hard (quantifiable) data and soft (qualitative) data. Even then, metrics are necessary but not sufficient. Boards are above all human places and rely ultimately on human judgment to deliver their ends.

To make competent judgments requires the capabilities of those around the boardroom table to be optimized. That means having a system to assess and track those capabilities. However, most boards have neither any form of systematic capability identification nor one of appraisal. Even when these do exist, they tend to be superficial. Too many chairmen and directors rely on sensing the immediate while avoiding hard facts and confrontation, especially about personal performance.

Chapter 6 listed the hierarchy of board information: corporate performance, board performance, and director performance. These indicate the various inter-related measures that the board must continually monitor to fulfill its primary duty of balancing the directoral dilemma of showing the way ahead while giving prudent control. What processes and measures can be used to ensure the professionalization of boards of directors?

Board Evaluation and Appraisal

The first step must be to create a system of benchmarking individual and group capabilities, then to ensure at least annual appraisal against these, both for each board member and for the board itself as a separate legal entity. The techniques for board appraisal are no different from any other appraisal system: identifying key performance areas (tasks) and agreed value-based behaviors (processes) that reinforce the business's purpose and vision, developing a system for assessing them, and doing it regularly and rigorously.

However, the constructive micro-political climate in which open board appraisal takes place can initially be difficult to create, and is often tricky to sustain, unless there is total commitment to it from the chairman and the directors. Board evaluation and appraisal involve levels of trust and confidentiality around the boardroom table that take a significant investment of time and openness to reach. Most board directors have big egos. So if appraisal is to be seen as an investment by those directors, what is in it for them?

The ultimate answer is protection—of their personal (family) wealth, of their reputation in their professional career and in their community, and ensuring freedom from jail. Most of all, the development of directoral competence and appraisal gives the highest of prizes: the protection and growth of personal integrity. Following the amoral and immoral 1980s and 1990s, integrity is re-establishing itself as a key stabilizing factor in many directors' lives. Given the alarming rise of litigation in western democracies, many directors will see directoral competence building and appraisal—the professionalization of directing—as their key form of protection.

At present, the fight in most corporations is to get even a basic competence-based appraisal system in place. It is a source of continuing wonderment to me that virtually all corporate training and development budgets, in terms of both time and money, cut out before they reach board level. There seems to be a naïve international wish to believe that directors must know what they are doing because they were selected for the job. Therefore, the logic goes, on election directors become omniscient. They will know all about what is going on both within and without their organization and how best to exercise their accountabilities.

The huge majority of the evidence shows the opposite. People elected to become directors rarely have any guided induction or inclusion processes, let alone systematic directoral competence-building. They flounder and, not wanting to ask for help for fear of looking foolish, simply stick to the comfort of their old functional specialities and hope to pick up the broader, directoral stuff as they go along. This rarely happens, so when there is trouble in the boardroom they tend to drop out (unofficially) of the power game and their behavior reverts to their old executive "position of comfort." If they were previously executives within the company, they will take back all of their old job (albeit unofficially). If they are nonexecutive directors, they will seek to muscle in on their speciality in this organization, or will drop out, again unofficially.

Both sets of behaviors create two major organizational issues. First, the reversion to specialist behavior creates friction with the existing executives in the organization. Turf wars break out, much heat is generated, and the more junior executive has to ratchet down to the job below them—with subsequent negative knock-on effects on costs and motivation throughout the organization. Second, if organizational capability surveys are conducted, it is often found that even senior people complain of being paid to do a job one or two levels above the work they actually do. This is organizationally both ineffective and inefficient. But worse is to follow—who, then, does the true directoral work? Enter the all-powerful managing director and sometimes the chairman.

This is not a satisfactory state of affairs. The simple allocation of time and money budgets to board and director training and appraisal has fast and highly cost-effective impacts on board competence, which positively affects the whole organization. Remember that the last of the ten directoral duties is the duty of learning, developing, and communicating. This assumes that any director must not only be trained to a high standard but must continue with their learning and annual appraisals throughout their career to ensure their continuing professional development.

Who is responsible for assessing the competence of the board and the individual directors? Of this there is no legal doubt—the chairman of the board. However, this can be news to many chairmen. They assume that somehow the managing director and the major shareholders will have some (undefined) processes for doing this and therefore that the chairman should stay well out of it. Wrong: The chairman is legally responsible for the competence of the board, and increasingly needs to demonstrate to the owners the processes by which he ensures this.

The basis of a board appraisal system

The best appraisal systems have two things in common:

❖ A common set of *behaviors* derived from the company's value state-ment. These "value-based assessments" are very powerful as they set a common standard across the company, and so can be used as much for the chairman as for the weekend security guard without changing any of the behavioral dimensions. If they have also been developed with staff input, they will be seen as fair, egalitarian, and, importantly, energizing.

❖ A common *tasks* framework so that the delivery of task-based per-formance (the specific work done to deliver a specific job) also has an agreed common basis.

Applied to the board these define its competences—the agreed mix of attitudes, knowledge, and skills needed to deliver the essential direc-toral roles and tasks.

The simplest system of board and director appraisal consists of five elements:

❖ A review of the self-disciplinary processes of the board—essentially its self-control mechanisms—that give its unique "emotional climate."

❖ A review of its working processes—especially in terms of its over-all budgeting of its time and the development of its competences—to deliver the four aspects of the learning board model effectively.

❖ A review of its directoral dashboard, its future income-generation and prudent control mechanisms.

❖ A review of the values used in delivering the learning board demands, specifically in line with the ten directoral duties spelt out in Chapter 4.

❖ A review of the overall performance of the business and the board's specific contribution in adding shareholder value.

These are all measurable. A score for the effectiveness of the board as a working group of colleagues can be derived from them, together with the board's development needs. From the same information the scores of each director can be determined, as can their individual development needs.

One very simple way of constructing the "tasks" side of the board appraisal is first to benchmark the "self-management" aspects of board procedure. Then add the four learning board quadrants—policy formulation and foresight, strategic thinking, supervising management, and accountability—and take each subset within these to create a checklist. The third step is to use the ten directoral duties as the "behaviors" side of the appraisal.

This checklist can become the source document for a confidential and, if found necessary, anonymous 360-degree board appraisal system that will include:

❖ Chairman review.
❖ Peer review.
❖ Direct report review.

It can incorporate a simple scoring system to help identify areas of:

❖ Superior performance.
❖ Over-performance.
❖ Acceptable performance.
❖ Under-performance.
❖ Poor performance.

It must also include an agreed development plan for both the board and individual directors in terms of a time and money budget.

Blockages to the board appraisal processes

There can be major problems in launching board appraisals. One is anger on the part of some directors at the sheer effrontery of the thought that they may benefit from a competence appraisal. They argue that they must be OK or they would not be in post; the "experience has taught me enough" argument. But what "experience"? If, as is common, they have only answered questions on their single functional discipline, what have they learned about the totality of direct-ing? If they are relying on their external network—the "I have been Secretary of State, therefore I will rely on my contacts and so know everything I need to know" argument—how do they address the spe-cific needs of this organization? Or are they mere ciphers nodding to the rhetorical questions of the managing director and chairman while window-dressing the board? Like the Bourbons, do they learn nothing and forget nothing, even though they have sat on the board for ten years?

Rather than argue the rational case for appraisal, I sometimes sim-ply "benchmark" such directors. The deal is that if they can answer correctly five of the six "quick quiz" questions (page 70), they do not have to proceed with any form of basic training but instead rely purely on group and personal development processes. In my 25 years of prac-tice no one, including legal counsel, has succeeded in getting five cor-rect answers.

Chairmen and nonexecutive directors are often seen as difficult to appraise. They are not. All directors must be treated equally in the appraisal system as they are equal under the law.

A frequently asked question is: "If you are using a 360-degree sys-tem, how can you appraise the chairman?" I have had to do this on occasion. For example, the chairman of a leading retail bank was under some shareholder pressure for better corporate performance. He had also agreed to have a 360-degree appraisal as a public symbol of his support for the launch of such a system across the whole bank, involving well over 100,000 employees. He was apprehensive about his own appraisal, but felt that he must be seen both to undertake and to benefit from the process otherwise his commitment to the massive financial investment in staff appraisal was likely to be questioned by shareholders at the forthcoming AGM.

I briefed him on the options and he decided not to have a 270-degree appraisal (he joked that he reported only to God), but a full 360-degree one. To ensure this we invited individuals from some of the major shareholder groups (fund managers) and a few outspoken customers and suppliers to complete, anonymously, the 360-degree circle. This was a great success and some very rich data was generated.

The problem then was not with the chairman but in giving open, although confidential, feedback on his scores to the board and a few senior, direct-report executives. The chairman was keen to do this and to relate his perceived strengths, weaknesses, and developmental needs as seen by the others and himself. However, while the non-executive directors were happy to join in the open discussion, the executive directors proved silent (and very fearful). It took a great deal of work by the chairman and myself over the following hour to create the conditions under which sufficient trust was generated that there would be "no reprisals" on the executive directors before they would open up.

Once we did get underway the endeavor went very well and the chairman later published a concise version of his development needs to the whole organization in their newspaper, and asked for help if staff saw him over-doing, or under-doing, certain unhelpful behaviors around the organization. This gave great credibility to the total corporate appraisal process. But it also taught the chairman just how all-powerful he was seen to be by his fellow directors—and how careful he must be in future to ensure that he was not encouraging self-censorship or mind-guarding among them. He found it a useful yet humbling process.

Developing the Content of Board Training

An effective board appraisal process will obviously point to the need for training and development for the individual directors. Two new notions are sweeping through director and board development thinking. First, that simply replicating the functions of executives at a higher functional level is not a solution but a key part of the present problem. Second, that there is now significant demand for the accreditation of directors—directing is becoming an assessable profession.

The present problem with much of director development is that if any board training has been done, it tends to replicate the functional divisions of the executives, sometimes with the twist of "from the director's viewpoint." So we still see cheap and cheerful mini-MBAs being taught to directors, often in the classroom, using the functional areas of accounting, human resources, strategy, marketing, production, procurement, service delivery, etc. This is not helpful.

In future the development of director and board competences will need to be very different: less MBA fixated (focused on analytical and managerial specialisms) and more focused on developing professional directors (on the key, active, integrative processes of directing). At Board Performance Ltd[1] we are developing the essence of the "professional director" by integrative processes, which include:

❖ Effective board working.
❖ Living the legal roles, tasks, and accountabilities of the board.
❖ Formulating policy.
❖ Developing strategic thought.
❖ Assessing risks.
❖ Effective board decision-making.
❖ Implementing and learning from strategy.
❖ Funding.
❖ Delivering the triple bottom line.
❖ Overseeing organizational change.

This would be a radical shift for most directors, especially those who assume that they can coast comfortably to retirement on their previous functional achievements. The list above also makes some rigorous assumptions:

❖ Boards of directors will accept and become much more active in their key role of driving the enterprise forward while keeping it under prudent control.
❖ Boards will be paid properly for their work.
❖ Boards will budget sufficient time to be able to deliver their roles and tasks.
❖ Executive directors will be paid a separate director's fee equal to that of any other director.
❖ All directors will need induction, inclusion, and training.
❖ All directors will need rigorous and regular appraisal.

❖ All directors need a personal development plan.
❖ The board will need its own development plan.
❖ Time and money budgets will be made available by the board for its own development.

This list is both necessary and sufficient to launch a board and director development process that will have at least a sporting chance of succeeding. If one or more elements are missing, the chances of success are reduced dramatically.

The Chartered Director Initiative

I am pleased to have been part of a small team of director volunteers and staff members based at the Institute of Directors, London who have created the award of Chartered Director.[2] This unique qualification is based on a written examination and a subsequent oral examination concerning a minimum of five years' full (nonfunction-specific) directoral experience. Success in both, plus signing a code of conduct and agreeing to a monitored system of continuing professional development, leads to the award, made through the UK Government's Privy Council.

The first 150 directors have graduated and as well as UK directors from large and small, private and public-sector businesses, they include Singaporean, US, Belgian, and Dutch citizens. That this is not merely of British interest is shown by the fact that the Japanese Management Association came to London and negotiated a major Chartered Director program tailored to their specific needs, while maintaining the integrity of the UK's approach.

The Chartered Director program has a multiple-choice examination covering the areas of:

❖ The role of the company director.
❖ Finance.
❖ Business strategy.
❖ Marketing.

❖ Organizing for tomorrow.
❖ People mean business.

These will soon be supplemented by:

❖ Board decision-making.
❖ Directing change.

Some academics and other professional bodies were extremely skeptical that all of this could be covered in a three-hour written examination, however carefully designed. Nevertheless, some of the doubters were invited to sit the examinations as an experiment and found them tough—very tough. An MBA did not help them much as the view needed for the exam is from the boardroom, not from the executive group.

After passing the examination a candidate is asked to prepare a detailed portfolio of their directoral work over a five-year period. This has to be countersigned by the relevant colleagues and chairmen before the oral examination, which is conducted by trained and experienced director interviewers. Again, this is seen to be tough and some candidates are "referred," typically until they have broadened their boardroom experience away from purely functional disciplines.

Technically, the accreditation process is a public examination agreed by the Privy Council, not by IoD London who administers it and runs training through its Centre for Director Development. People can walk in off the street and sit the exam, although this is not advised as no such person has ever passed. However, many people have passed using distance learning and sat the examination abroad with the British Council invigilating. Many countries, particularly in Asia and Africa, are looking at how to adopt and adapt the Chartered Director process.

This form of accreditation is still in its early learning phase. I hope that it will develop so that the total content is based on directoral thought and action, i.e., that it will drop the old functional approach (finance, marketing, etc.) and focus on individual director and board performance. Even in its present state it excites me as a highly constructive way ahead. The need to train and develop both boards and directors is now so acute that the question is no longer "whether?" or "when?" but "how?"

Epilogue

The Board of the Future

PICTURE THE SCENE... It had been a very messy and difficult time, but the new board felt that it was finally in a position to direct the business fully. All of the 12 directors (whether they had previously been executives or outsiders) had now been through their "rite of passage" training to become full directors. Under the careful supervision of the chairman they had successfully completed their rigorous induction, inclusion, and directoral competence-building programs. These allowed them to concentrate now on adding shareholder value in three ways: through the development of the board itself as an effective workgroup, through developing their personal abilities to become competent directors, and through better ensuring that the whole company was based on adding shareholder value.

Seven of them (including the younger "high-potential manager" who had not been through the executive director route) were completing their Chartered Director programs. They were joking with the others about having better and cheaper directors' and officers' liability insurance cover as well as being seen as much more credible to both the owners of the business and fund managers, and, with their new US acquisition, much less likely to end up in jail for 20 years with a $5 million fine. In addition, they realized that such accreditation also gave them a much bigger incentive to act professionally with integrity—to deliver what they had promised to the shareholders, customers, and staff through honest dealing and transparent behavior. Their business's longer-term future had begun to look increasingly attractive, particularly as it had successfully renewed its national and international license to operate in a number of European, Asian, and African countries, as well as the US.

Nevertheless, it had been tough. Driving out the old board's "country club" mindset had been harder than expected. This was because it had pervaded the whole organization rather than just the board, and had placed great power in the hands of the senior executives, who had proved very reluctant to hand directoral power back to where it right-fully belonged. However, growing shareholder discontent with the old regime had been very helpful, and the decision by two of the "shareholder activist" fund managers to "name and shame" the old board was the final straw in their removal. The outgoing directors were not happy, but took some perverse comfort in the fact that they held some of the last valid stock options granted in the "greedy nineties." The rest had to accept that the rules of the direction-giving game had changed for ever, and that from now on their lack of accountability, lack of questioning skills, lack of strategic thinking, lack of risk assessment, and dereliction of duty in board decision-making had all been publicly spotlighted. They had to go. They had no defense, even though some had been executive directors of other listed companies, and others were members of the great and the good. It had been uncomfortable on all sides, but necessary.

The sequence that triggered the board changes was becoming increasingly common in companies. The leading shareholders had demanded a board evaluation review because of the business's con-tinuing under-performance, and insisted also that whoever com-prised the new board should start with a conscious board assessment and development process. The evaluation was handled in two ways. First, there was an overall review of the board's struc-ture and internal processes to check its effectiveness as a working group to deliver the business's purpose, vision, and values, and to monitor the external and internal environments effectively. Second, there was a review of the competences of each director, including the chairman, to ensure that there was sufficient diversity to enable them to fulfill their risk-assessment and decision-taking directoral roles. This latter review looked first at the range of practical and wider social experiences of those around the boardroom table, and then at their individual preferences in the areas of idea generation, leadership and development styles, conflict resolution, and decision-making, to ensure that they could formulate policy and think strategically.

This data was then compared with the total board scores to give the foundation of a board renewal plan. On the basis of this data only one of the old directors was kept and the specifications for the new directors were developed. As these people would be holding the business in trust for the shareholders, leading shareholders were also involved in the discussions on director specifications. These personal and board evaluation criteria were seen as onerous at first, especially when set in the context of the business performance requirement to turn round the company within 18 months. Nevertheless, they were seen as necessary for the board to generate business policies and strategies that added to shareholder value at a rate of 15 percent every three years. Most people in the industry laughed and said that this could never be achieved.

It was. This was mainly through careful selection of the new directors—as proper directors with separate directoral contracts and fees, and separate executive contracts where appropriate. The selection process was aided greatly by access to the database of Management Diagnostics Ltd, which allowed scanning of all the directors of listed companies in Europe and the US and careful questioning of their track records, movements, bonuses and options related to share price movements, etc. Each was recruited with a desire to be part of a "new wave" board that would be seen as a role model for the professionalization of directing. They were committed to the company's purpose based on the concept of added shareholder value.

The directors then set out to gain a full understanding of their board roles, to evaluate the board's and their personal development needs, especially to take the executives out of an exclusive focus on their specialist roles, and to agree appropriate development plans. These were set in the context of the ten directoral duties and learning board models. They plotted an 18-month total board development process starting with a reaffirmation of the company's purpose, vision, and values, and the use of an organizational capability survey to give benchmark figures on company culture, sources of energy for driving change, and ability to implement strategy.

In addition, they agreed to a regular rhythm for the board's year, defining carefully which were essentially "administrative and information-receiving" meetings, and which were idea-generating, strategic thinking, risk-assessing, and strategic decision-making meetings. The latter were put into every board member's diary a year ahead and their individual inputs agreed on which areas of the external world they would monitor during each quarterly period, and to which of the functional elements within the business they would give oversight. Both perspectives were part of a carefully designed board risk-assessment process.

The board year started with a policy formulation "awayday," then went into a mixture of monthly directoral dashboard information, especially trend line, "numbers" meetings (which the chairman kept rigorously to no longer than an hour per month) and at least quarterly strategic thinking awaydays (often spread over two or three days). This was the board's core process and allowed executives and outside specialists to join the directors and enrich their debates. Ensuring the commitment of executives was essential both to implement the agreed strategies, and to give rapid and accurate feedback on the rollout so that the board could learn the consequences of their decisions quickly.

The board's annual cycle had a crucial awayday in the ninth month of the financial year. This was the accountability-checking meeting. With so many new regulations and the move from civil to criminal litigation in so many cases involving boards and directors, it was now essential to check that all accountabilities were on track, rather than hurriedly to post-rationalize them at month 13, as had been done in the old days.

This feedback was not merely on financial matters. Very early on the directors had taken the bold decision that in the light of increasing shareholder activism and growing stakeholder-driven legislation, they would adopt the "triple bottom line" approach for their reporting stance. So they appointed separate auditors for their financial, physical environmental, and corporate social responsibility reports to the owners, and ensured that these were measured carefully against the board's targets announced at the beginning of each year. To their surprise, very few of the shareholders moaned at the likely extra costs. Most knew through their internet chatrooms that public opinion and new legislation were both moving firmly in this direction. Indeed, many commented that taking an active triple bottom line approach gave them confidence that the board was looking ahead and giving leadership—a very different stance from the old board. It was seen especially to enhance the business's previously dented reputation, while creating long-term value for the owners. The first annual report in the new mode—*Generations, Globe, and Gains*—was very well received internationally and is now being talked about, and used, as a model for others. More importantly, it has been of great help in having the organization placed on the "preferred partners" lists of many corporations, governments, and agencies. This has already allowed it into bidding in two countries where previously there had been significant barriers to entry.

The board's development process has been simple, but not easy. The evaluation "benchmarking" processes have gone well and are now accepted practice both for the present board and for any new director. Even the chairman has found it useful and it helped him establish his credibility with the board, the executives, and the shareholders. The process itself identified some major gaps in the personal development needs of many directors. It also helped raise, spotlight, and rapidly resolve the inevitable role, task, and personality clashes between the chairman and the managing director, and between the directors and the executives. The joint production of the document on the reserved powers of the board was crucial to resolving such problems. The development of a directory of directors' interests also helped build the shareholders' trust in the board.

A further important part of the board development process was the careful thought given to the related budgets for their time and money. Their individual and group development was recognized as critical to the effectiveness of the entire business. While many had felt curiously guilty about this at the start, it is now accepted as fundamental to the business's success. Now the board feels competent at direction-giving and is accepted as such by both shareholders and brokers. It is also ready for the "board renewal" process so that it can keep itself refreshed.

When all is said and done, the board's key focus is on the straightforward concept that its role is to drive the business ahead while keeping it under prudent control. In the end, being a board member is that simple—and that profound.

Notes and References

Overture

1   Throughout the book I use the word chairman since that is the one most commonly employed, but I am not by any means trying to imply that everyone in this position is male.

2   I had hoped to call this book *Behind the Boardroom Door*, but that title has been reserved by my colleague Bob Tricker, to whom I defer as the originator of the modern term "corporate governance" in his book of that name. The title *Thin on Top* came from a cheery, boisterous brainstorming session at the Association of Management Education and Development's (AMED) Director Development Network and I am grateful to Jennie Kettlewell for generating it. It captures my concerns clearly.

Chapter 1

1   www.lens-inc.com.

2   Adolf A Berle & Gardiner C Means (1968) *The Modern Corporation and Private Property*, Harcourt Brace, New York (original edition 1932).

Chapter 2

1   Nevill Coghill's modern rendition (Penguin, London, 1951) is:
    This gentlecock was master in some measure
    Of seven hens, all there to do his pleasure.

    "Never again, for all your flattering lies,
    You'll coax a song to make me blink my eyes;
    And as for those who blink when they should look,

God blot them from his everlasting Book!"
"Nay, rather," said the fox, "his plagues be flung
On all who chatter that should hold their tongue."

2   Bob Tricker (1983) *Corporate Governance*, Gower, Aldershot.

3   The Cadbury Committee (1992) *Report of the Committee on the Financial Aspects of Corporate Governance*, Gee, London.

4   The Greenbury Committee (1995) *Directors' Remuneration: Report of a Study Group*, Gee, London.

5   The Hampel Committee (1998) Committee on Corporate Governance: Final Report, Gee, London.

6   London Stock Exchange (1998) *The Combined Code: Principles of Good Governance and Code of Best Practice*, Gee, London.

7   The Turnbull Report (1999) *Internal Control: Guidance for Directors on the Combined Code*, Institute of Chartered Accountants in England and Wales, London.

8   HM Treasury (2001) *The Myners Review of Institutional Investment*, HM Treasury, London.

9   *King Report on Corporate Governance for South Africa* 1994 and 2002, www.iodsa.co.za.

10 *CACG Code of Good Practice for the Board*, available from the Commonwealth Business Network, combinet@combinet.net or g.bowes@xtra.co.nz.

11 Leon Levy (2003) *The Mind of Wall Street: A Legendary Financier on the Perils of Greed and the Mysteries of the Market*, Texere, London.

12 *Financial Times*, January 25, 2002.

13 *Financial Times*, June 13, 2002.

14 *Financial Times*, February 21, 2002.

15 www.iod.com.

Chapter 3

1   Chris Pierce (ed.) (2000) *The Effective Director*, Kogan Page, London.

2   Berle & Means, *op. cit.*

Chapter 4

1 *CACG Code of Good Practice for the Board*, op. cit.
2 www.transparency.org.
3 www.soros.org/osi.
4 www.citizen.org/trade.
5 Turnbull Report, *op. cit.*
6 P Rutteman *et al.* (1994) *Internal Control and Financial Reporting: Guidance for Directors of Listed Companies Registered in the UK*, Institute of Chartered Accountants in England and Wales, London.
7 Myners' Report, *op. cit.*
8 *IoD Standards for the Board*, Institute of Directors, London, www.iod.com.
9 Institute of Directors (2001) *The Company Director's Guidelines: Your Duties, Responsibilities and Liabilities*, Kogan Page, London.
10 Charles Handy (1990) "What are companies for?," speech at Royal Society of Arts, London, December.
11 www.tomorrowscompany.com.
12 *People, Planet and Profits*, www.shell.com.
13 www.bp.com.
14 www.ftse4good.co.uk.

Chapter 5

1 Francis Fukuyama (1996) *Trust: Social Virtues and the Creation of Prosperity*, Touchstone, London.
2 Reg W Revans (1982) *The ABC of Action Learning*, Chartwell Bratt, Lund.
3 W R Ashby (1956) "Self-Regulation and Sufficient Variety," in *Introduction to Cybernetics*, Wiley, London.
4 Charles Handy & Roger Harrison (1976) *Understanding Organisations*, Penguin, Harmondsworth.
5 Robert Burns, "To a Louse," 1786.
6 P F Drucker (1999) *The Frontiers of Management: Where Tomorrow's Decisions Are Being Shaped Today*, Penguin, New York.
7 Bob Garratt (1996) *The Fish Rots from the Head: The Crisis in our Boardrooms*, Profile, London.

8   *CACG Guidelines for Corporate Governance, op. cit.*
9   *Strengths Deployment Inventory*, available from PSP4SDI@compuserve.com.
10 Irving Janis (1982) *Groupthink*, Houghton Mifflin, New York.
11 www.ibe.org.uk.

Chapter 6
1   Clive Morton (1998) *Beyond World Class*, Macmillan Business, London.
2   Bob Garratt (2000) *The Learning Organisation*, Profile, London.

Chapter 7
1   Michael Shermer (1998) *Why People Believe Weird Things: Pseudoscience, Superstition, and Other Confusions of our Time*, W H Freeman, New York.
2   *The Fish Rots from the Head*, op. cit.
3   *The Learning Organisation*, *op. cit.*; Bob Garratt (2001) *Twelve Organisational Capabilities: Valuing People at Work*, Profile, London.
4   R S Kaplan & P Norton (1996) *The Balanced Scorecard*, Harvard Business School Press, Boston, MA.
5   European Foundation for Quality Management, www.efqm.com.
6   J L Heskett, W E Slasser, & L A Schlesinger (1997) *The Service Profit Chain*, Free Press, New York.
7   www.securityforum.com.
8   Tony Buzan (1993) *The Mind Map Book: Radiant Thinking*, BBC, London.
9   Edward de Bono (2000) *Six Thinking Hats*, Penguin, Harmondsworth.
10 *Thinking Intentions Profile*, www.effectiveintelligence.com.
11 Bob Garratt (ed.) (1994) *Developing Strategic Thought*, Profile, London.
12 Michael Porter (1980) *Competitive Advantage*, Free Press, New York.
13 *Ibid.*
14 Turnbull Report, *op. cit.*

15 Gerry Johnson (2001) *Exploring Corporate Strategy*, FT Prentice Hall, London.

16 Max Boisot (1998) *Knowledge Assets: Securing Competitive Advantage in the Information Economy*, Oxford University Press, Oxford.

17 Gary Hamel (2000) *Leading the Revolution*, Penguin, Harmondsworth.

18 A Brandenberger & B Nalebuff (1996) *Co-Opetition*, HarperCollins Business, New York.

19 *Twelve Organisational Capabilities*, op. cit.

Chapter 8

1 www.boardperformance.com.
2 www.iod.com.

Useful Contacts

AMED Director Development Network
www.amed.management.org.uk

African Management Services Company (AMSCO)
charles.minor@amscobv.com

Asian Corporate Governance Association
Jamie@acga-asia.org

Board Performance Ltd
www.boardperformance.com *or* info@boardperformance.com

Bob Monks
www.ragm.com

Commonwealth Association for Corporate Governance
g.bowes@xtra.co.nz *or* michael.gillibrand@commonwealth.org

Corporate Governance Journal
www.blackwellpublishing.com/monks/journal.htm

Corporate Library
www.thecorporatelibrary.com

Corporate Watch
www.corpwatch.org

Centre for Tomorrow's Company
www.tomorrowscompany.com

Foresight Management Group
www.globalcoaching.com.au

FTSE4Good
www.ftse4good.co.uk

Global Watch
www.zmag.org

International Corporate Governance Network (ICGN)
www.icgn.org

Institute of Business Ethics
www.ibe.org.uk

Institute of Directors, London
www.iod.com

Institutional Shareholder Services
www.issproxy.com

OECD Corporate Governance Principles
www.oecd.org

Organisation Development Ltd, Hong Kong
www.odlgroup.com.hk

Organisational Development Ltd, Singapore
v_ram@osl.com.sg

Pension & Investment Research Consultants (PIRC)
www.pirc.co.uk

The Success Group (Director Coaching)
www.thesuccessgroup.co.uk

Transparency International
www.transparency.org

UK Cabinet Office,Corporate Governance
www.cabinet-office.gov.uk/risk/Corporate_Governance_Folder/
Corporate_Governance_Guidance.htm

General Corporate Governance Websites

Global Corporate Governance Forum
www.gcgf.org/index.htm

US Corporate Governance Links
www.calpers-governance.org/links

European Corporate Governance Links
www.ecgi.org

Corporate Governance Codes

International Codes and Principles
www.ecgi.org/codes/menu_international.htm

European Corporate Governance Codes and Principles
www.ecgi.org/codes/menu_europe.htm

American Corporate Governance Codes and Principles
www.ecgi.org/codes/menu_americas.htm

Asia-Pacific Corporate Governance Codes and Principles
www.ecgi.org/codes/menu_asia_pacific.htm

South Africa Corporate Governance Codes and Principles
www.ecgi.org/codes/country_pages/codes_south_africa.htm

Index

A

B

GEC 5, 45
Germany 44, 89
Gillibrand, Michael 82
Global Crossing 129
Global Trade Watch 91
goals, of board 150
Goldsmith, Peter 83
governance, beginnings of 33–4
Grade, Michael 69
gray surfers 53
greed 1, 3, 4, 13, 75, 123
Greenbury Committee 38, 98
Greenpeace 53, 54
Greenspan, Alan 4, 20
Grubman, Jack 124
Guinness 34

H

Hamel, Gary 199
Hampel Report 38, 98
Handelsbanken 149
Handy, Charles 106
Headdon, Christopher 47
health, corporate 150–52
helicopter view 154, 184
Hermes Pensions Management
    50–51, 52, 104
Hewlett-Packard 11, 17
Higgs Report ix–x, 40
HIH 154
Hill & Knowlton 187
honesty 3, 54, 92, 94–6, 104,
    198; *see also* probity
humility 3

Huntingdon Life Sciences 54
Hurn, Sir Roger 46

I

idea generation 188–92, 220,
    222
importance of corporate
    governance 28
inclusive company 106
incompetence
    directoral 1, 12, 44, 48, 49, 85
    strategic 1, 3, 41, 44, 47, 150
independent directors 18, 39, 40,
    66, 69
    appointment of 40
induction of directors 1, 27, 70,
    85, 101, 215, 219
information
    due diligence 185–8
    inputs 182–5
Information Security Forum 186
Inno-Pac 154
Institute of Business Ethics 135
Institute of Directors 63, 68, 76,
    112, 216–18
insurance, directors' and officers'
    liability 13, 47–8, 60–61, 67,
    112, 219
integrity, personal 30, 132, 133,
    209
International Monetary Fund 56

T

X